THERE IS NO SUCH THING AS

BUSINESS LEADERSHIP

Scott M. Carter

Scott M. Carter Publishing

Forest Lake, Minnesota

Scott M. Carter/Scott M. Carter Publishing

Forest Lake, MN 55025

www.scottmcarter.com

Book Layout ©2017 BookDesignTemplates.com

Cover Design selfpubbookcovers.com/Dmick27

Ordering Information:

Quantity sales. Special discounts are available on quantity purchases by corporations, associations, and others. For details, contact the "Special Sales Department" at the web address above.

There Is No Such Thing As Business Leadership/ Scott M. Carter. —1st ed.

ISBN 979-8-9879170-0-8

Back To BASIC™ book series

There Is No Such Thing As Business Leadership

Back To BASIC™: Acting In Leadership

The Bible Teaches Acting In Leadership

Leadership: Achieving Optimal Effectiveness

Contents

Thank you to my incredible wife Lisa, my family, and my friends who support my efforts to continue writing with a focus on serving others. Thank you to everyone who inspires me to act in leadership and thank you to my readers who support my works.

There is no such thing as business leadership. There is only leadership in its true essence. ~Scott M. Carter.

We get a lot of things wrong!

1500 years ago, people thought the earth was flat. I'm not kidding you. People thought you'd fall off the edge if you traveled too far. We still see this mystical mindset portrayed in movies. My wife, Lisa, and I love the Marvel comic series. In the film *Thor*, Asgard is the capital of nine fictional realms. When in Asgard, a person can fall off the edge into space. Watch your step.

500 years ago, people thought the sun and the planets in our solar system revolved around the earth. If you challenged that thought, those who ruled might put you to death for heresy. In 1543, Nicolaus Copernicus detailed his theory of the universe in which the earth and other planets rotated around the sun. People referred to Copernicus as radical. Acceptance of his idea by society required a long-term fight, taking more than a century.

People think villagers in Salem, Massachusetts burned people at the stake for witchery. In 1692, during the witch trials, twenty people lost their lives. Of those twenty, the colonial authorities hung nineteen and tortured one. Today we understand that what appears to be magic or witchery consists of science we do not yet understand. No one was burned at the stake. Today when you use science, no one accuses you of being a witch.

People think Michael Jackson invented the moonwalk. Moonwalking consists of illusionary footwork that makes it appear like a person slides backward when walking. People moonwalked as early as the 1930s. The oldest recording I could find is of Bill Baily at New York's Apollo Theater in 1955. Jackson did not invent it.

In the epic biblical battle between David and Goliath, people think David was the underdog. Most people who write about this epic matchup tell the story wrong. Goliath was the underdog. David had a tactical advantage. The fight was quick and one-sided. Due to increased knowledge and insight, we can more accurately tell this legendary tale.

While growing up in the 1970s, my family saw Goliath go toe to toe with other combatants dozens of times. How is this possible? The American Wrestling Association, AWA, first aired on tv in 1972. I was eleven years old. We attended the eleven o'clock church service every Sunday and promptly returned home by noon. The minute we walked in the door, we turned on the tv. We went to church, sat in the front row, listened to that week's sermon, then rushed home to watch grown men beat each other up on the boob tube. That's what we called it in the 1970s. If you spent too much time in front of the tv, you were considered an idiot, a boob. Imagine three boys and their dad gathered around the tv watching weekly matchups between wrestlers with names like "Mad Dog" Vachon, "Butcher" Vachon, and Ray "The Crippler" Stevens.

We each had our favorite we loved to cheer for. I waited each week in anticipation of seeing a tag team match, hoping that "Jumping" Jim Brunzell would be part of the line-up. My dad's favorite was "The Crusher." During one of his interviews, "The Crusher" hung a dented folding metal chair around his neck, held a beer in one hand, and a cigar in the other. He represented the working man's man. No matter who we loved to watch, each week would be filled with anticipation to see what crazy antics might come next.

Then one spectacular Sunday, the emcee of the AWA, "Mean Gene" Okerlund, introduced this behemoth of a man. We watched in awe as this man stepped over the top rope to enter the ring, and then he sat on that very same rope. For most wrestlers, the upper rope lined up with the middle of their rib cage. This guy was sitting on it. It was the craziest thing we'd seen up to that point, and we had witnessed some weird stuff. Who was this eighth wonder of the universe? Andre "The Giant."

Andre stood seven feet, four inches tall, weighing five-hundred forty pounds. Mean Gene astounded the viewers with size comparisons between himself and Andre. Andre wore a size twenty-two shoe, and when Andre held his hand next to Mean Gene's head, Andre's hand could wrap around Okerlund's skull. In one interview, Andre took a ring off one of his fingers, and Mean Gene slid a half dollar through it. Folks, those are some big fingers. Andre spoke with a deep, commanding voice accompanied by facial features that made him look menacing. What caused Andre to be this intimidating giant? Andre had acromegaly.

Acromegaly, a rare condition where the body produces too much growth hormone, causes body tissues and bones to grow abnormally in size. Side effects of acromegaly can include a speech impediment and impaired vision. Andre "The Giant" could have been Goliath. A baritone voice, massive in size with incredible strength and a terrorizing look about him, would make all men recoil from facing Goliath in combat. Would you go up against him in a real battle resulting in death?

The *Bible* says that Goliath stood six cubits and a span, equaling a little over eleven feet tall. Other ancient texts say his height reached four cubits and a span equaling about seven feet nine inches. We don't know which is correct, but we do know that Robert Wadlow, who died in 1940, the tallest man on record, was eight feet, eleven inches, and suffered from acromegaly.

Because we can view photos of Robert Wadlow and action videos of Andre "The Giant," we can vividly picture what it would be like standing face to face with Goliath. He'd be huge, covered in the best armor, wielding a spear and sword that looked small in his hands, like a grown man playing with a child's version of these weapons. Goliath would be virtually unbeatable when well-trained in up close and personal hand-to-hand combat. However, David also possessed battle-worthy strengths. Those strengths served an entirely different purpose; protecting his flock.

Movies often provide some reality of how armies fought battles centuries ago. However, just as often as they correctly depict those battles, the filmmakers also leave out incredible and fascinating parts of history. Centuries ago, armies trained and used slingers. These slingers were deadly. How deadly? In 1981 Larry Bray set the world record for a stone cast with a sling. He achieved a distance of 437 meters, a little over four football fields.

A well-trained slinger at close range can hit a person in the head with great accuracy. The small rock exiting the sling has the velocity of a bullet from a handgun which can penetrate the pelt of a large animal or a person's skull. Historical records exist illustrating important battles won because of slingers. Have you ever seen these incredible slingers in a movie scene? I haven't, either.

Imagine yourself living 3000 years ago as a shepherd tending your flock of sheep. You're not eleven feet tall, or even eight feet in height, but more likely just over five feet. On average, people who lived centuries ago were shorter than we are today. Most shepherds were not large menacing men trained to do battle, yet their livelihood depended on keeping their flock safe.

Imagine you're the shepherd, and dangerous predators lurk about attempting to steal your flock. How do you protect them? You can't hop in your car and run down to the local store and buy a gun, crossbow, or any other items we would have today, and you certainly aren't going toe to toe with such predators. What would you do?

Well, shepherds used slings. Slings were light in weight, easy to reload, and, as we now know, quite deadly. We know that Goliath would be massive in size, be well-trained, and have the best armor and weapons. David would be average, two to three feet shorter in height, and have a sling tied to his waist. Who would you bet on to win? Hold that thought. Before we get to the contest between David and Goliath, we must know why David and Goliath fight in the first place. We learn that David would have to win another battle first.

In ancient times, battles between large armies might be decided using the best man of each army in a one-on-one contest. Rather than hundreds of men dying in battle, one life would be lost. This head-to-head competition would determine who wins without a full-on clashing of armies ensuing. Hundreds, if not thousands, of soldiers might live and go home to their families. The story of David and Goliath exists because of a war between two armies.

One army belonged to the Philistines and the other army to the Israelites. These two armies were stuck in gridlock, positioned on opposing sides of a valley. Because of the valley and terrain, the army who attempted to attack the other side would be at a tactical disadvantage, so neither side advanced. During this standoff, the Philistines sent their great warrior, Goliath, down into the valley to taunt the Israelites.

King Saul ruled over the Israelites. Saul would be the person who decided whether to send their best warrior to stand against Goliath or choose a full-on battle between the two armies. Imagine you're King Saul, and this menacing giant is taunting your entire army. No one steps up to fight this behemoth of a man. The King certainly isn't going to send someone he thinks doesn't have a high probability of winning. If he loses, he and his army fall under the rule of the other King.

At this point, David enters the scene. David lived under the rule of King Saul. With the help of David's brother and others who were soldiers in Saul's army, David gets an audience with the King. David offers to fight Goliath. The thought of an untrained shepherd boy fighting this behemoth of a man covered in menacing armor? Why, *simply ridiculous*. At least, that's what any sane person would utter.

I often wonder what those conversations looked like because, after much deliberation, King Saul gives David permission to enter this battle that would determine the fate of many men. This decision would seem odd to those not involved in that conversation.

Then David continues to surprise and confuse the King. David also refused to wear any armor or take any of the traditional battlefield weapons of the time. Imagine the King and other men sitting around thinking, "this boy be crazy!"

As David approaches the space in the valley where the fate of both armies will be determined, Goliath cannot see David very well. Goliath has blurred vision, a side effect of acromegaly, a detriment to his greatness as a warrior. We know this because the Bible tells us how Goliath is yelling, "Come close." Goliath needs his opponent right in front of him to see him more clearly. When David gets close enough so Goliath can at least get a decent look at him, he discovers a shepherd boy without armor, carrying only a walking staff. Goliath becomes angry and says, "Am I a dog that you come at me with sticks?" Goliath is insulted by the presence of someone he deems unworthy to do battle against him.

On the other hand, David sees Goliath as no more menacing than the predators attacking his flock. He has faced this battle countless times. He is no rookie. David has taken down creatures perhaps scarier than Goliath because of their speed and agility. We know that a sling can throw a small stone over four football fields with the velocity of a handgun. How close did David need to get to Goliath? One hundred or two hundred feet away? Fifty feet away?

Due to his size, Goliath would be slow-moving and non-threatening to David at any of those distances. David takes out his sling, slides a stone into the little pouch, and whirls it around with tremendous centrifugal force. He releases the stone that penetrates Goliath's skull, dropping this massive, intimidating warrior to the ground. David then walks over, takes Goliath's sword, and cuts off Goliath's head. It's a good thing this is not how the matches ended in the AWA when people faced Andre "The Giant." Our after church Sunday experience would have been quite different.

We get things wrong. We have for centuries, and we will continue to do so. Experience and insight continue to allow us to correct a few of those things. The earth is not flat, the sun does not revolve around the earth, and David wasn't an underdog.

What's next?

You, the reader, will soon discover that we have been telling the wrong stories regarding the concept of leadership. If you were asked, "what is leadership?" could you answer with any level of certainty? If you were given the task of defining leadership, could you accomplish that task? And when asked how you came to that answer, could you prove why your definition is correct?

We are two decades into the twenty-first century and now have the knowledge and insight to get leadership right. I provided you with a new perspective on the battle between David and Goliath. When you finish this book, you'll have a completely new viewpoint on the concept of leadership. You'll discover how we misguidedly attached leadership to a position in a hierarchy and linked leadership to "doing business." Because we did that, we tell the story of leadership wrong. You'll learn that leadership does not revolve around a position in a hierarchy, just as the sun does not revolve around the earth, and most of what you know are fads and clichés. You will discover that there is no such thing as business leadership; there is only leadership in its true essence. Are you prepared for this journey of new insight?

CHAPTER ONE

Madoff, Jones, and Delvey

Madoff

Bernard Madoff, known as Bernie by his business associates, was born in 1938 in a lower-lower-middle-class neighborhood in the boroughs of Queens in New York. Bernie grew up with his brother Peter. Both worked hard and faced the same childhood struggles as many people do. As a lifeguard and sprinkler installer, Bernie saved a few thousand dollars. Then collaborating with his brother Peter, they took that work ethic and determination to wall street. By the 1980s, the entity of Bernard L. Madoff securities occupied three floors of a mid-town Manhattan high-rise. Two struggling kids from the Borough of Queens had made it. Nothing unusual about any of this story. Writers present stories like this to us all the time in leadership books. It all sounds very leaderly.

Madoff kept going and used his expertise to help launch Nasdaq, the first electronic stock exchange. When you see Nasdaq on the news, Bernie played a crucial role in creating that platform and eventually became the chairman of that exchange. We jump forward to 2008 when Madoff pleaded guilty to orchestrating a massive Ponzi scheme for over a decade and a half. How massive? A deceptive plan that wiped out $17 billion in savings from unknowing victims. These days we talk in billions like it is nothing because we have started talking in trillions. Let's put this in perspective. That's like taking the annual gross income of $40,000 from 425,000 families. Many of the victims were very successful charities and organizations whose sole purpose was to help those in need, and many of these organizations were utterly wiped out.

Jones

James Warren Jones was born May 13, 1931, in Crete, Indiana. During his youth, Jones became a regular churchgoer. He graduated from Butler University and entered the ministry. In 1955 Jones established the Wings of Deliverance, a Pentecostal church known as the Peoples Temple. During this time, he worked with the homeless, was a vocal proponent of racial integration, and in the early 1960s, he served as Director of the Indianapolis Human Rights Commission.

Jones had built a congregation, a group of churchgoers. For several decades Jones had substantial influence over others. Then things took a hard left turn.

Jones adopted the name "The Prophet" and became obsessed with wielding his power. Soon there were allegations of illegally diverting members' income to himself for his personal use. Those allegations drove Jones and his followers to Jonestown, Guyana, located near the small town of Port Kaituma, on the border of Venezuela.

On November 18, 1978, through both fear and false incentives, the cult members drank poison and died under his persuasion. This mass suicide was no little event. Over 900 people, including 300 under the age of 17, perished that day.

Delvey

Anna Delvey, whose real name is Anna Sorokin, was born on January 23, 1991, in Domodedovo, Russia, a little town outside Moscow. She and her brother were raised in a middle-class family; her father drove a truck, and her mother once owned a small convenience store. By 2013 Anna had made her way to New York City, working for Purple Magazine. She decided to make New York her home. However, a career in publishing is different from what Anna desired. She desired fame.

For years, Sorokin paraded as a wealthy German heiress to infiltrate the inner circle of some of the city's most well-known socialites. To accomplish her goal of fame, she scammed hotels, banks, and the people she so passionately wanted to become. Under her new moniker, Delvey, she proved to be a resourceful and brilliant woman who came up with ideas to further her fictitious brand. One such idea included the Anna Delvey Foundation, a private club and art foundation.

On April 25, 2019, Sorokin was found guilty on eight charges, including grand larceny in the first degree, grand larceny in the second degree, and grand larceny in the third degree. Anna consulted on the making of a Netflix series called Inventing Anna and has had books written about her. Delvie achieved her pursuit of fame.

The BASIC™ Leadership Challenge

I intentionally selected these three stories. The Madoff story involves a for-profit business entity, the Jones story falls under the social sector label, and the Delvey story is about an individual looking for fame.

You, the reader, have just been put in charge of a leadership program. Your objective is to define leadership and create a leadership training program. You have been given the option to look at leadership from two different perspectives. Under both options below, how would you define leadership? How would you use these three stories to help you?

Option 1: You get to draw from everything that exists about the concept of leadership and use it to define leadership.

Option 2: You get to start from scratch. Under the premise that everything we know about leadership, everything you've read, heard, or watched about leadership up to this point, does not exists.

At the end of this book, you will be invited to participate in *The BASIC Leadership Challenge.*

In the following chapters, you will experience the journey I took to address leadership from both perspectives. Look at this journey as participating in a leadership coaching workshop. I will provide enough material to assist in getting you started in your endeavor to define leadership. Let's begin by learning about the Loop of Optimal Effectiveness and then applying the concept of leadership to the loop.

CHAPTER TWO

The Loop

The Loop of Optimal Effectiveness illustrates how complexity, once it reaches a certain level, hinders our effectiveness. The loop also sets the premise that, in some cases, extreme complexity is absolutely essential to achieve optimal effectiveness. This illustration of how complexity impacts effectiveness is so simple that once you see it, you'll give yourself the V-8 slap to the forehead and utter the famous catchphrase from the cartoon character Homer Simpson, *Doh!*

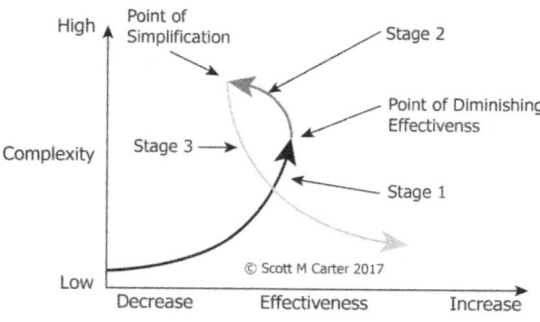

Loop of Optimal Effectiveness

The three stages.

1. Stage One: As the level of complexity rises, the level of effectiveness begins to taper off, and at some point, the level of effectiveness has peaked and is no longer increasing.
2. Stage Two: From that point, when the level of complexity continues to rise, our ability to be effective can decrease. We go backwards.
3. Stage Three: The only way to begin to move forward toward increasing effectiveness is to decrease the complexity.

Computers and the Loop

Experts initially thought that computers would help us reach levels of success never seen before. This premise is true, to a point. But for optimal effectiveness, computers and computer programs had to go through all three stages.

As the computer advanced, so did the programs associated with them. We can now take programs such as Excel and create formulas to quickly track and analyze numerical data. Computers and computer programs allowed us to do this more quickly, and we became more efficient and effective at rapidly analyzing data, at least initially.

As we became more proficient in using these new tools, we also expanded the number of ways we analyze data. We calculated percentages and ratios, created projections and forecasts, and overanalyzed the crap out of everything. The programmers added more options like creating pivot tables, charts, and graphs.

As the number of features climbed, we added more and more things we wanted to analyze, calculate, and present in prettier and fancier ways. The complexity and effectiveness begin to follow the curve in the first stage. The number of things we analyze and the multiple formats in which we present the data increased to the point where the data points we analyze began to provide conflicting information.

We then found ways to manipulate the data to show success where success doesn't genuinely exist. Confusion and distrust both rise as well. We have hit the second stage of The Loop of Optimal Effectiveness, and our ability to be effective diminishes. What do we end up doing in business? We decide which data points will help us go in our desired direction, and then we limit ourselves to those data points. We simplify so we can optimize our effectiveness—a straightforward principle.

Complexity, Good or Bad?

Using the loop as our guide, we will also learn that an extreme rise in complexity is not necessarily a bad thing. Moving through the first two stages can be essential for achieving optimal effectiveness.

Imagine it's 2015, and your organization realized that it had upwards of 2,000 KPIs, Key Point Indicators, for tracking data. How would you know which ones helped you the most? How would you know if any of them are in direct contrast to each other?

Sky is an organization that uses neural networks to analyze customer feedback data and provide insight to companies regarding their customer's experiences. Imagine you're the head of Sky and you begin working with an organization, discovering that they had 2,000 KPIs. How confusing would it be to accurately analyze any data? This confusion occurred with one of Sky's partners, PepsiCo. The head of research and analytics, Aji Ghose, along with his team, cut that 2,000 number down to 30.

Here's the critical question. Would the research team have the same 30 final KPIs if they only had 100 KPIs at the time they decided to reduce the number of data points? How about 500 or 1,000? We do not know. However, because an excessive number existed, would the final list they create be more effective than if they had half as many? They could use the insight gained from an excessive level of complexity to decide which ones would help them achieve their goals most effectively. We surmise that having that extreme complexity allowed them to achieve maximum effectiveness in choosing their final 30.

Organizational Charts and the Loop

We tend to create massive, confusing organizational charts and produce excessive amounts of procedures. What do experts recommend? John Kotter is the Konosuke Matsushita Professor of Leadership, Emeritus, at the Harvard Business School. Kotter's book *Accelerate (XLR8)*, published in 2014, shows us how an excessive number of processes and procedures create too much complexity in our organizations. When we combine that complexity in processes and procedures with our massive organizational charts, they develop a level of complexity that hinders our ability to be effective. The conclusion reached by experts is that it restricts our capacity to innovate and achieve high levels of engagement.

Kotter outlines how organizations begin small, with very few rules and procedures, where innovation is high. Due to the high level of innovation, they achieve tremendous growth. Then as they become larger and larger, rules and regulations multiply and begin to stifle the innovation that allowed them to achieve accelerated growth in the first place. The organization gets bogged down with layers of red tape and all the bureaucracy, rules, and things we cannot do rather than things we can do. We build an organizational chart with layers and layers of managers and executives, and only a tiny handful of people understand how this happens.

Kotter provides a perfect example of enacting a solution to begin the third stage of the Loop of Effectiveness. He tells organizations to move away from complex processes and procedures and reduce the focus on complicated organizational charts. He is not saying to eliminate organizational charts or processes and procedures, but to begin reducing the complexity to increase the effectiveness in affecting change and our ability to innovate in organizations.

Galls' Law

John Gall was an author and pediatrician who wrote about systems theory. He is best known for *Gall's Law*. From his work, we know two things with a high level of certainty.

I.   A complex system that works is invariably found to have evolved from a simple system that works, and

II. A complex system that works poorly is invariably found to have evolved from a simple system that worked well.

Everything Follows the Loop

All things, including the concept of leadership, follow the loop's pattern, eventually leading to a rise in complexity.

✓ When a concept or process is first discovered, it can exist in an elementary form.

✓ We can increase the effectiveness of a concept or process because we gain insight through its use. In all cases, the complexity rises along with its effectiveness (stage one).

✓ We continue to build on the concept or process, expanding the terms and steps until it reaches that point where effectiveness stops and perhaps even begins to lose effectiveness. The complexity hinders the effectiveness (stage two).

✓ We can take the over-abundance of knowledge and experience we have on the concept or process, and we can simplify to a level that is now much more powerful than the simplicity of the original concept or process (stage three).

The Result

The result is that we now have a concept or process that can be as simple as where we began. But more...

➢ meaningful and concise,

➢ easily understood,

➢ and more effectively used.

Therefore, in some cases, the power of the loop lies in reaching the point at which an extreme rise in complexity hinders effectiveness. Moving through the first two stages of the loop can be essential in creating an optimal level of effectiveness. What do you think we might discover when we apply the concept of leadership to the loop? Read the next chapter, then decide if you think we are in stage one, stage two, or stage three when it comes to the concept of leadership.

CHAPTER THREE

Leadership and the Loop

When did the concept of leadership enter the scene regarding business and organizations? What resources would help us make that determination? Could you answer those two questions with any high level of confidence?

It's January of 2016, and what ended up being a three-year journey lies before me. I just didn't know it yet. After decades of living in the corporate world and still frustrated at the stupidity that seemed to take hold in the organizations where I worked, I set a goal of writing a platform that could address the abundance of what appeared to be insane behaviors in defiance of common sense and logic. That project would take a hard left turn when I began addressing the concept of leadership.

Have you ever searched for the definition of leadership? What actions, behaviors, beliefs, etc., do leaders exhibit? Attempting to answer those questions would take me on an enlightening journey filled with twists and turns.

My bookshelf at home differs from what we see in most leadership videos on YouTube. In those videos, in the background, we typically see a nicely laid-out collection of books, all having the same binding and matching color. It's a marketing strategy for visual effects implying that the person in the video is highly educated and intelligent. My collection looks significantly different—all sizes and colors, devoid of extensive matching collections.

I researched the concepts of leadership and management from 1890 to 2019, a 130-year span of time, using three criteria.

1. Number of resources on leadership and management,
2. Access to the resources (how would people get their hands on those resources, assuming anyone read them at all), and
3. Content and type of the resources (theory or science-based, and research paper or book).

My collection includes books such as Henry Ford's *My Philosophy of Industry*, published in 1929. It's an original copy, not a reprint. The paper it is printed on is quite different than modern books. I tried to get my hands on what I thought were the most relevant to addressing the complexity associated with the concept of leadership, and in their original first print edition.

I dug into the works of Peter Drucker, Warren Bennis, Abraham Maslow, Bernard Bass, Douglas McGregor, Dale Carnegie, Fred Fiedler, Frederick Taylor, Henry Mintzberg, W. Edwards Deming, John Kotter, Max Weber, Napoleon Hill, and Ralph Stogdill.

Those names represent only a tiny smattering of what I read from a long and distinguished list of those who addressed either leadership, management, or both from 1890 to 2019. That is what my bookshelf looks like, a cornucopia of management, leadership, and personal development books.

Leadership: The Rise in Complexity

I chose 1890 as the starting point because 1890 to roughly 1915 represents the most significant increase in the industrialization of any country or civilization in recorded history. This significant increase isn't speculation. It comes from experts such as Gary Hamel, who has been on the faculty of the London Business School for more than thirty-five years. Hamel writes for the *Harvard Business Review* and studies the concept of management. Yes, industrialization occurred before 1890, but different from this. Many of the terms and innovations that we have today sprang from this massive industrialization period beginning around 1890 and well into the 20th century.

For instance, the term CEO, Chief Executive Officer, was invented during this period. Taylorism, the time and motion study of efficiency created by Frederick Taylor, brought management science to the factory floor. Henry Ford applied Taylor's time and motion concepts to excel at mass-producing automobiles, leading to the use of assembly lines. Taylor, Weber, and Fayol created our current business structure consisting of bureaucracy, administration, and management in that same time frame. Everything accelerated from there, including both management theory and leadership theory. Management came first.

As the industrialization of the United States pushed forward, the majority of the studies and theories were about management. In 1967, Fred Fiedler published his book, *A Theory of Leadership Effectiveness*. He tells us about the rise in theory studies regarding leadership. One study per year in the 1930s, rising to 150 studies per year in the 1950s. Most studies consist of something referred to as a white paper, resembling a college thesis paper or something similar. On average, only seven people read a white paper study; one is probably the author's mom. We laugh because that's true. Write any paper, even a crappy one, and your mom will tell you it's awesome.

The third criterion of my study, content, and type of resources (theory or science-based, research paper or book) comes into play here. The 1960s, 70s, and 80s begin the rise in books about leadership that more people are likely to read. The issue with most of these resources is that they took language from the studies of theories containing language that tied leadership to the top positions in organizational hierarchies and pushed it forward. That happened because people studied organizations attempting to understand the concept of leadership through the behaviors of those at the top. People used "businesses" as their study subjects.

When I laid out the resources that addressed management and leadership, then looked at the number of those resources, how a person might access them, and the content and type, the concepts of management and leadership followed the loop—staggering amounts of complexity leading to diminished effectiveness.

The concept of management is an invention. Until I began my research, I had never heard anyone talk about the invention of management. Have you heard top speakers address it? Gary Hamel does. Leadership is also an invention. Management and leadership are both inventions and distinctly different. Management is a position in organizational hierarchies. Leadership is not a position anywhere. We already had and still have titles for all positions within hierarchies. We'll address that in the next chapter.

Leadership Definitions and Labels

By the time we hit 1985, in his book *Leaders*, Warren Bennis tells us that the number of leadership definitions and labels had accumulated to over 800. Bennis held the title of The Joseph Debell Distinguished Professor of Management and Organization at the University of Southern California School of Business Administration.

Bennis wrote 27 books on the subject, spanning decades until he passed in 2014. While most of us are mere "readers" of leadership theories, Bennis and others were neck-deep in leadership studies and theory. He interacted with organizations and participated in debates on the development of educational platforms in academia. Bennis' books were snapshots in time, providing insight along the leadership development journey.

In 1974 Ralph M. Stogdill Produced the *Handbook of Leadership: A Survey of Theory and Research.* This book is the granddaddy of leadership books. This book's first versions contain 429 pages, with 150 pages providing over 2,800 resource references. By the third edition in 1990, this book is a massive 914 pages of copy, with 190 additional pages containing over 7,500 resource references. That's almost double in size from its first publication in 1974. We see complexity surrounding the concept of leadership rising at an accelerated rate. What do you think the number of leadership definitions might be today?

Now that you have a better understanding of the excessive complexity surrounding the concept of leadership go ahead and complete a search for the definition of leadership. Most of those definitions resulted by attaching the concept of leadership to doing business and a position in hierarchies. Not only do we get a massive number of definitions, but we also get conflicting and contradictory definitions and labels. It's no wonder everyone is so confused.

Do you operate under participative or authoritarian leadership? Transactional or transformational leadership? Ethical or unethical leadership? Autocratic or democratic leadership? Do you practice humility leadership or shame leadership? Do you operate under confident leadership or arrogant leadership? And it gets worse. Then we began using management and leadership together in business. When are you managing, and when are you leading? Suppose we want more leaders who act in leadership, and leadership is a position in a hierarchy. In that case, we're in deep doo-doo because the number of top positions in hierarchies is extremely limited.

So now what? That was the question I said aloud to myself as I wrapped up my research. At the end of chapter one, your objective was to define leadership under two options. Let's revisit those options.

> Option 1: you get to draw from everything that exists about the concept of leadership and use it to define leadership.

> Option 2: You get to start from scratch. Under the premise that everything we know about leadership, everything you've read, heard, or watched about leadership up to this point, does not exist.

Under option one, more than enough information exists to take a shot at defining leadership. Could you? Or better yet, would you even want to try? How confident are you that you would be right if you did? Would your definition add to the complexity or simplify it? Could you test your definition to prove it's viable, no matter what people throw at it?

If you decide to pass on option one, that leaves option two, starting from scratch. Where would you begin? In the following few chapters, you'll see how I approached this project and how I achieved the objective of defining how and when a person is acting in leadership, thereby being a leader at any given moment in time. And you get to put it to the test. The good news is that I promise not to bore you. This is not a research book; it is an enlightening adventure story about the concept of leadership. I will, however, have to warn you.

Warning!

Warning: Only go further with reading this book if you are prepared to handle the consequences of the knowledge written within. After you finish, when you hear or read phrases such as "Leadership is influence" and "To be a leader, a person needs followers," you will cringe. This book will ruin everything you think you know about the concept of leadership. Read on only if you are of strong mind and will.

CHAPTER FOUR

Title Me This, Title Me That

First, all books that illustrate studies of organizations tell us about business strategies. They tell us about the business plans implemented or not implemented. Those strategies and business plans either helped or hindered the growth of an organization. All of these stories about organizational entities illustrate hindsight of past decisions. None provide us with any organization's "future" strategy or plan. The authors who discussed organizations did not write about leadership; they wrote about past business decisions.

Government, churches, and non-profits are businesses and organizations. None are exempt from competing in the marketplace. Cities compete against each other to entice people to live there, as do all fifty states in the USA. They compete for your tax dollars. Other countries compete against each other, persuading you to vacation in their magical worlds and offering incentives for organizations to establish a business there. The FBI and CIA compete against each other for the responsibilities of protecting our country and money allocated from congress so they can continue operating. Non-profits compete against one another for your donations. No matter their form or structure, everyone competes in the marketplace. And in every case, whether we call it a corporation, business, organization, or social sector businesses such as non-profits, those entities all have a hierarchy, and those hierarchies all have existing titles.

In business, we have CEOs, Chief Executive Officers, Presidents, and Vice Presidents, aka Executives. We have Directors, Managers, and a list of other titles for each layer within the organizational chart. We have a Board of Directors, not a board of leadership.

Titles existed in hierarchies before the industrialization of the United States began. There were Kings, Queens, Lords, Knights, and Peasants. We have priests, pastors, bishops, Reverends, and ministers in the religious sector. We call a Japanese Zen Teacher a Roshi. You've probably heard the title, Dalai Lama. All cultures have titles in their hierarchies.

For sports fans seeking knowledge about leadership, we hear how much coaching styles matter. Coaching styles are not leadership styles. What do coaches do? They coach. Trainers train, and players play. Sports hierarchies already have titles.

In the military, we have Generals, Lieutenants, Majors, Captains, also called Officers, and on and on. In government, we have a President, Senators, Congressmen and Congresswomen, Governors, Mayors, and on and on.

Have you ever seen an employment ad listing "leadership" to describe a position in a company's hierarchy? No, the ads are for CEO, President, Director, and Manager because we already have names for all the positions in all organizational structures. Have you ever seen an employment ad for followers? No, because we have laborers, workers, privates (for the military), and other names for those on the front line. Yet we have people creating Ted Talk videos telling us that the one thing you need to be a leader is followers. Then why is no one hiring followers? Does anyone else ask these questions, or am I alone here? "Bueller? Anyone?" If you didn't get that reference, how about, "Hello, hello, anybody home? Hey, think McFly."

Ask the right questions.

Making sure we ask the right question is more important than looking around the room to see if we have the best answer. As a society, we have been conditioned to think that "answering the question" is the primary objective. The problem is that we never stop to ensure we are asking the right questions.

> *"We're so worried about wanting to be the person with the right answer that we never stop to make sure we are asking the right questions."* ~Scott M. Carter

I created a list of responsibilities using language currently associated with organizational charts. You fill in the blank with the title of the person responsible for making these things happen. Read through the two paragraphs, then come back and fill in the blank with the title.

The _____ encourages learning behavior by rewarding people when learning happens. Rewards can include promotions, increased compensation, recognition for excellence, and expanded responsibilities.

The _____ encourages innovation, critical thinking, and experimentation. A shared commitment to the organization's objectives, and adherence to the corporate values, while promoting shared knowledge between departments must be uplifted as part of the mission.

If you are like most people, you filled in the blanks with one of several executive titles depending on what size organization. CEO, Owner, President, Director, and Manager are common choices. The people who wrote the books using that language are attempting to attach leadership to a position in a hierarchy, so they used the words leader and leaders to fill in the blank. Those two paragraphs define the potential responsibilities of a person at or near the top of an organization, not when a person is acting in leadership or a leader.

If you are an engineer, you perform engineering. If you are a surgeon, you perform surgery. If you are an accountant, you perform accounting. Executives execute business plans, directors direct and coordinators coordinate business activities, managers manage production numbers and metrics, and laborers labor.

Now, please tell us how a CEO performs leadership. They don't. That person is the Chief Executive Officer. They oversee the other executives, keeping the department heads on track with the corporate objectives and vision. Executives execute a plan focused on achieving a goal or desired outcome. The CEO drives an organization's major decisions, direction, and culture. A director directs others toward attaining a desired goal or outcome. You can execute a plan, but you cannot leadership a plan. One can direct or manage people, but one cannot leadership people.

Please, go leadership something. I *triple-dog dare you.* Yep, I went right to the triple dog dare. When we notice something that doesn't quite make sense, we correct it. One cannot secretary something. That is why most companies no longer use that title. We have assistants that assist or support professionals that support people. Those titles more clearly illustrate what a person in that position does.

Leadership is not a position in any hierarchy. None of the positions in any hierarchy have anything to do with leadership except that a person can act in leadership, thereby being a leader at any given moment while holding that position. Leadership and any position in any hierarchy are distinctly different. If leadership is not a position in any hierarchy, then what is it?

Leadership is not a position in any hierarchy. None of the positions in any hierarchy have anything to do with leadership except that a person can act in leadership, thereby being a leader at any given moment while holding that position. Leadership and any position in any hierarchy are distinctly different. ~Scott M. Carter

BASIC™ Leadership Platform

Suppose we went back through resources consisting of books, white paper studies, or any other format addressing the concept of leadership. Could we identify a series of main components that help us define leadership? In chapter four, we learned that asking a compelling question is more important than focusing on coming up with the best-sounding answer. The opening question of this chapter, chapter five, is not the right question. We're asking if we can define leadership, and we're limiting ourselves to a very short time frame.

First, the study of the concept of leadership started and grew during the mass industrialization of the United States. Second, we weren't studying leadership; we were studying decisions made by those who held positions at the top of hierarchies, including business, politics, and societal structures. We should be asking, "what constitutes acting in leadership?" When I asked that question, the answers showed up.

To answer that question, we can go back to the early philosophers and the writings of the *Bible*. We can go as far back in time as we'd like. After looking at everything humans have compiled, would the puzzle pieces appear organically? Like the law of gravity and other laws that helps us understand the natural order of the universe, does a natural set of components exist that define "acting in leadership?"

The answer is, "Yes." Seven components help us define when a person is acting in leadership—Belief, Action, Success, Insight, Collaboration, Integrity, and the Leadership Lifeline. Let's begin with the first five components that make up the outer ring of what I have coined as the BASIC™ Leadership platform.

Belief

Holy duck dung Batman, we can go down some never-ending rabbit holes of complexity. I researched the difference between beliefs and mindset. I'll spare you the lost in space feeling from that insane road trip. Instead, please put me on a roller coaster ride with a belly full of pizza, tacos, ice cream, and soda. We all know how that ride will end, yet a belly-filled roller coaster disaster would be more fun than another research project decerning the difference between some synonyms.

A synonym is a word or phrase that means exactly or nearly the same as another word or phrase in the same language. I took one for the team by researching synonyms for dozens of words associated with the information that is about to follow. For our first component, we can talk in terms of attitude, opinions, disposition, our philosophy, mood, mindset, and a slew of other labels, and it all leads back to beliefs. For the first component, "beliefs" won hands down. Beliefs encompasses all of the synonyms listed above and is the first of the initial five elements of our BASIC Leadership platform.

Believing in something will not make it true. However, people will act or not act based on what they believe. Believing defines and creates our lives. We see it everywhere in modern times and back to the early philosophers.

Walt Disney knew this and helped us to act on it. *The Wonderful World of Disney* first aired on October 27, 1954. In 1961 it moved to NBC so people could see it in color. "The following program is brought to you in living color," the voice on our tv would proclaim. Children across the nation would smile and wriggle with anticipation as they viewed the fairytale castle engulfed in fireworks while the magical Disney tune played. That same image and music are still used today at the beginning of all the great stories that Disney creates. Walt tells us to use our imagination. He inspires us first to believe.

When you believe in a thing, believe in it all the way, implicitly and unquestionably. ~Walt Disney

In 1937 Napoleon Hill published his book *Think and Grow Rich*. The primary premise of his book? Our beliefs. Money, fame, power, contentment, peace of mind, and happiness are ours when we begin with our beliefs. Hill uses the term "think" because rational thought is also part of what he teaches, but we must start by believing first. Read his book, and you'll find that beliefs are the underlying driver for a person's actions. Here are just a handful of quotes related to beliefs.

> *But when you ask, you must believe and not doubt because the one who doubts is like a wave of the sea, blown and tossed by the wind.* (James 1:6 NIV)

> *To believe in something and not to live it is dishonest.* ~Mahatma Gandhi

> *The energy of the mind is the essence of life.* ~Aristotle.

When Aristotle refers to the energy of the mind, he refers to the power of a person's beliefs.

> *Reality is created by the mind; we can change our reality by changing our mind.* ~Plato

Plato understood that when our beliefs change, our reality changes.

> *You have the power over your mind – not outside events. Realize this, and you will find strength.* ~Marcus Aurelius, Emperor of Rome

One of the most powerful emperors of Rome understood that our strength comes from our mind, our beliefs.

I could go on with hundreds of references, but those will suffice. I can say to myself, "I believe there is more out there, so I continue to search. Or, I do not believe there is more out there, so I do not search." It's that simple. For humans, any action taken, or not taken, is based on some belief. That brings us to our second component, action.

Action

> Knowledge without action is wastefulness, and action without knowledge is foolish. ~Al-Ghazâlî

Al-Ghazâlî was one of the most prominent and influential philosophers, theologians, jurists, and mystics of Sunni Islam.

If you plan to present the argument of, "Well, I didn't act; Therefore, the action component doesn't hold water," that would be a misguided belief. Not taking action is still taking action. It is the same as if two choices were put in front of you, and you decide not to choose either of those options, you have still made a choice. The third choice is the action of not making a choice. Most people need to learn this simple principle. Not taking action is still taking action. That action is to do nothing. We are always taking some sort of action, even if that action is to do nothing.

The Canadian Rock band Rush produced a song called "Free Will." Their lyrics tell us that if you decide to do nothing, you have still made a choice. For heaven's sake, rock stars get this right, yet entire societies seem to be lacking in the understanding of these simple concepts.

Heaven knows that before I began my research, I lacked the understanding. Most people have come to believe rock stars consist primarily of pot smoking, drug-induced partiers chasing groupies. Ok, some do, but did you know that Brian May, the legendary guitarist of Queen, has a Ph.D. in astrophysics? His knowledge of physics was partly responsible for Queen's extraordinary sound. How about Gene Simons of KISS? Well-known for a tongue that can probably clean out the bottom of a peanut butter jar, Simons has a teaching degree. He dominated his competition when he participated in one of Trump's Apprentice tv episodes. Tom Morello of Rage Against the Machine has a BA in political science. That may be why they are considered one of today's most politically active bands.

Now, back to our regularly scheduled program. I go on little rants now and then. The point is, taking no action is still taking action.

Be as you wish to seem. ~Socrates

Be the kind of person that you want people to think you are. ~Socrates

Those two statements from Socrates illustrate how our first two components, beliefs and action, work in conjunction with each other. Your actions must mirror your beliefs. You are required to act to make it a reality.

And I tell you, ask, and it will be given to you; seek,
and you will find; knock, and it will be opened to you.
(Matthew 7:7 NIV)

Everything in Matthews's quote requires action. And
a person's incentive to take any of those actions is driven
by whether a person believes it can happen. Action
encompasses synonyms such as initiative, work, effort,
achievement, and endeavor.

Again, take a look at some leadership books or watch
some leadership videos, and you will find a cornucopia
of content telling us how leaders take action and how
leadership is about knowing when to act and when not
to act. Note that beliefs and actions do not require a
person to be in any position in any hierarchy, nor does
achieving success. However, taking or not taking any
action leads to success or non-success. Success is our
third component.

Success

When asking people to define leadership, you will
likely get hundreds of different answers. Ask a person to
define success, and you will get a similar result. The
complexity around the concept of success is also
staggering, with conflicting answers in direct contrast to
one another. However, just like defining when a person
is acting in leadership, there is an answer.

Our definition of success comes from Earl
Nightingale in his 1957 radio broadcast. Nightingale
defines success as "the progressive realization of a
worthy ideal." Success is not about some end goal.

Success comes from taking action or not taking action, and through a combination of unsuccessful and successful attempts, we continue to progress toward something. Success is an infinite journey toward whatever you decide is your worthy ideal. Small milestones, typically known as goals, exist along that infinite journey.

In 1986, James P. Carse published a book, *Finite and Infinite Games*. Simon Sinek, who wrote *Start with Why* (2009) and *Leaders Eat Last* (2014), takes Carse's concept and produces another book, *The Infinite Game* (2019). What does Sinek tell us? We must treat businesses like an infinite game. The worthy ideal is to ensure that the business continues, no matter who holds any executive positions in the hierarchy. Along that infinite journey, sometimes we will succeed and sometimes fail. Life and business are both infinite journeys, a progression. Therefore, Nightingale's definition best describes the concept of success.

We also tend to use negative language that is counterintuitive to creating a *take-action mindset*. The term failure has a negative connotation. A denotation is a dictionary definition. A connotation is an idea or feeling that a word invokes in addition to its literal or primary meaning. Failure creates a negative feeling causing a belief that there is no point in continuing. Change the language and approach, and you change the mindset, which can lead to continued action. Thomas Edison expresses the concept of success in such a way.

I have not failed. I've just found 10,000 ways that won't work. ~Thomas Edison

Edison was progressing toward a worthy ideal. Along that journey, he had successes and non-successes. Saying "other ways that won't work" does not have that same high level of negative connotation attached to it. That's the point of our definition of success. We don't fail. We experienced ways that didn't have the outcome we desired.

As humans, our thought processes, our ability to reason, and our fear of what others think easily overpower our desire to take action. Why? Because people care more about not failing than about succeeding. Let me repeat that. *People care more about not failing because of what others will think than they do about succeeding.* Squelch that fear by changing your definition of success so you can continue progressing toward a worthy ideal.

Progressive has synonyms such as consistency, continuous, increasing, developing, intensifying, and growing, to name a few. Each of these labels has become an individual type of leadership, driving the rise in complexity. Success is a progression. Our newly discovered definition of success helps us to simplify defining when a person is acting leadership.

Again, read some books on leadership or watch some videos. You will find that success is one of the central concepts consistently addressed. Take a look at the level of complexity, then try to define success. A common theme you'll notice is how "failure" is addressed.

Leadership is about continuing and learning, whether we are successful or not in any endeavor, big or small. We use those experiences to gain insight. Once we can clarify and define success, everything else falls into place. Nightingale defined success for us. We experience ways that do not produce the desired outcome, and those experiences provide insight. Insight is our fourth component.

Insight

Knowledge is simply information. Actions are merely actions. It is the insight we gain from both the information and our actions that matter.

> *For the things we have to learn before we can do them, we learn by doing them.* ~Aristotle

Aristotle understood the concept of gaining insight from learning and from taking action.

> *The one who learns and learns and doesn't practice is like the one who plows and plows and never plants.* ~Plato

To take action, whether reading to increase our knowledge or increasing our knowledge through taking action, when one does not intentionally use the insight gained from either, then you are just plowing without planting anything. Albert Einstein is attributed with saying, "Insanity is doing the same thing over and over and expecting different results." Insight only has value if we put it to use. Motivation without knowledge and insight is insanity.

Motivation alone is not enough. If you have an idiot and you motivate him, now you have a motivated idiot.
~Jim Rohn

We gain knowledge. Putting that knowledge to work gives us experience. Those experiences lead to wisdom. Gaining a better understanding impacts our perception, awareness, intuition, comprehension, and judgment. Gaining a better understanding can be a worthy ideal. Isn't this what we say leaders do? They seek insight, correct? We act on that new insight, and our beliefs can be impacted. Are you beginning to see how this all ties together? We use the word insight because its definition hits the nail on the head. Insight is the capacity to gain an accurate and intuitive understanding.

Knowledge is knowing that a tomato is a fruit. Experience tells us that it does not taste good in a fruit salad. Wisdom is knowing not to put it in a fruit salad ever again.

After covering four of the first five components, we can see the pattern that naturally occurs regarding synonyms. Beliefs encompass thoughts, mindsets, attitudes, opinions, and dispositions. Action covers work, effort, achievement, and endeavor. Progression encompasses developing, continuation, advancement, increasing, and growing. And now, insight covers wisdom, intuition, and judgment, to name a few. We have now reached the fifth of the seven components of the BASIC Leadership platform, collaboration.

Collaboration

Collaboration has become one of the most overused buzzwords in recent decades and is one of the most "made fun of" concepts, keeping pace with humorous quips about leadership. We tend to think of collaboration as something that occurs between two or more people. This mindset is a short-sighted point of view.

In the movie *Master and Commander: Far Side of the World*, the doctor on the ship, Stephen Maturin, played by Paul Bettany, is also a naturalist—a biologist whose interest lies primarily in the study of plants or animals. During a conversation with the ship's captain, the doctor shares the fascinating attributes of a bug that disguises itself as a stick to confuse its enemies. Captain Jack Aubrey, played by Russell Crowe, takes that new insight and acts on it. They disguise their warship as a vessel that hunts whales for profit. By doing so, they draw in their enemy and conquer them. While this may be a movie, collaboration with nature happens all the time in real life.

In 1928 Dr. Alexander Fleming returned from a holiday to find mold growing on a petri dish of Staphylococcus bacteria. He noticed that this mold was preventing the bacteria around it from growing. His studies showed that the mold produced a self-defense chemical that could kill bacteria. The name of that substance? Penicillin. The next time you visit your doctor to get a prescription, you'll know how that lifesaving drug came to be. Dr. Fleming collaborated with nature. You've gained insight into the history of penicillin.

In Japan, many rice growers have begun using ducks as a natural way to produce healthier crops. The ducks feed on insects and weeds without eating or harming the rice plants. As the ducks swim, their paddle-shaped feet oxygenate the water and stir up the soil, and their droppings are a natural fertilizer—a win-win collaboration with nature.

One would think this is something new, but it is not. Collaborating with ducks was an ancient rice-growing practice replaced by chemicals and machinery as technologies advanced. Just as chemicals and machinery replaced the natural partnership with ducks, we see how a position in a hierarchy replaced leadership in its true essence. We can gain insight from rice growers, illustrating how we need to get back to the basics.

We can collaborate with others without ever being in direct contact with them. I collaborated with many people who have written about the concept of leadership. I did so without ever meeting them or having a discussion with them. You and I are constantly collaborating. You just gained a more accurate and deeper intuitive understanding of collaboration. You did so by collaborating with me through this book. Your beliefs have likely changed, and you will now act or not act according to those new beliefs allowing yourself to progress toward some worthy ideal.

If everyone is moving forward together, then success takes care of itself. –Henry Ford

A plethora of collaboration quotes exist, from sports to business to life. Like Belief, Action, Success, and Insight, Collaboration consistently shows up in many resources. It encompasses synonyms such as teamwork, alliance, cooperation, and joint effort, to name a few. Let's recap the first of our five BASIC Leadership components.

The BASIC™ Leadership Outer Ring

> *Success is neither magical nor mysterious. Success is the natural consequence of consistently applying basic fundamentals.* ~Jim Rohn

The acronym BASIC stands for Belief, Action, Success, Insight, and Collaboration. BASIC illustrates the fundamentals of life, and the first part of acting in leadership.

> ➤ Belief—Trust, Faith, or Confidence in Someone or Something.
> ➤ Action—To Take Action; Do Something
> ➤ Success—The Result from Taking Action Toward a Worthy Ideal
> ➤ Insight—The Capacity to Gain an Accurate and Intuitive Understanding
> ➤ Collaboration—Joining with Someone or Something to Produce or Create

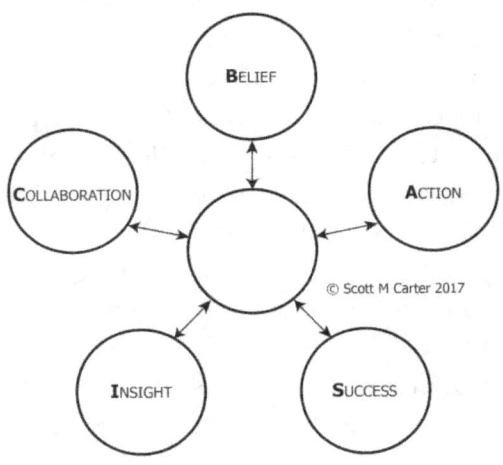

Back to BASIC™
Leadership Outer Ring

We now have the five components that make up the outer ring of the BASIC leadership platform. The question now becomes, how do we put them to use?

BASIC is a Wonkavator

In 1971 the movie *Willy Wonka and the Chocolate Factory* was released. Mr. Wonka, played by Gene Wilder, is the eccentric, kooky, brilliant creator of the chocolate factory. Spoiler alert! At the movie's ending, they get into a glass elevator, and Mr. Wonka says, "This is the great glass Wonkavator." Charlie's grandpa responds, "It's an elevator." Mr. Wonka corrects him and tells us, "It's a Wonkavator. An elevator can only go up and down, but the Wonkavator can go sideways and slantways, and longways, and backways, and squareways, and frontways, and other ways you can think of. Just press a button, and it takes you to any room in the factory." The BASIC Leadership platform works the same way as a Wonkavator.

When you've read as many books about platforms, theories, and systems as I have during my leadership studies, you run across diagram after diagram displaying circles, squares, and hexagons, generally arranged in a circle or oval. Most of these diagrams' common thread is that they follow a specific pattern. They start at point A, then to point B, then to C, D, E, and F. They put little arrows, sometimes with cool-looking arcs that show where you go next. They go in one direction. You cannot skip one component, jump across to some random element on the other side, or reverse. Or they have a two-option platform based on a yes or no answer to a question. Those platforms lack flexibility. Now that I've pointed this out to you, it'll leap off the pages (or computer screen), grab your snout, then squeeze it, making it honk like a clown nose. *Honk, honk.*

The BASIC leadership platform is a Wonkavator. You can move between the components based on what occurs naturally in any given situation. We've already experienced how this happens in the above explanations for each element. For example, when you gain more insight, it can move you in one or more directions. Your beliefs can be confirmed or changed. New insight can drive you to collaborate with someone or something different. The new understanding can cause you to take more action, or it may help determine if a non-success or success is moving you toward a worthy ideal.

This structure allows for things to occur naturally. Most patterns are limited, restricting our ability to be innovative and creative. BASIC is a vital structure that helps us begin to define when a person is acting in leadership. However, yes, there is almost always a however. The primary outer ring components of the BAISC Leadership platform structure alone are insufficient for determining when a person is acting in leadership. What you may have noticed in the BASIC Leadership diagram, there is a central hub you are required to pass through in order to move from one component to the next. What is this hub? It is the sixth component, integrity. Let's see what part it plays.

CHAPTER SIX

Values, Principles, Morals, Ethics, and Integrity

If someone asked you to explain the difference between values, principles, morals, ethics, and integrity, could you answer with a high degree of certainty? If you struggle, you are not alone. Most people struggle because these five things get jumbled, intermixed, and misunderstood.

In May 2018, Netflix released the series *Cobra Kai*, a spinoff 34 years after the *Karate Kid* movie trilogy. The Cobra Kai members live by a set of principles and values, as we all do. The members value "strike first, strike hard, no mercy." They operate under the principle of winning at all costs. The Cobra Kai are ok with any reputation bestowed upon them if they get to hold up the trophy to show they have won. They operate under that set of beliefs and chain of reasoning. When we watch the interactions in movies or mini-series like *Karate Kid* and

Cobra Kai, we have a natural sense of the contrast between right and wrong. To gain insight, let's examine the difference between values, principles, morals, ethics, and integrity.

- Values: 1. The regard that something is held to deserve; the importance, worth, or usefulness of something. 2. A person's principles or standards of behavior, one's judgment of what is important in life.

- Principles: A fundamental truth of position that serves as the foundation for a system of belief or behavior or a chain of reasoning.

- Morals: 1. Concerned with the principles of right and wrong behaviors and the goodness or badness of human character. 2. Holding or manifesting high principles for proper conduct.

- Ethics: 1. Moral principles that govern a person's behavior or the conducting of an activity. 2. the branch of knowledge that deals with moral principles.

- Integrity: 1. The quality of being honest and having strong moral principles; moral uprightness. 2. The state of being whole and undivided.

Choose One

Of the five choices above, which would you use as a test to determine if a person is acting in leadership?

When we gain insight, the answer becomes clear. Our choice is integrity.

Back to BASIC™
Leadership Platform

When moving from one component to another using the Wonkavator approach, we will always pass through the integrity hub to determine if we are acting in leadership. Let's clarify a few things.

We love complexity. The loop of optimal effectiveness tells us so. When applied to the loop, most concepts follow a path of complexity until they become less and less effective. We even do this when discussing and comparing values to principles or principles to morals. The level of complexity we can reach is insane.

Right and wrong are not subjective, and we know it. Because cannibals believe it is ok to kill and eat other human beings, it does not make that ritual valid. Cannibals eat people based on their values and principles. A person or society can act based on a set of principles or values, and not act with integrity. Also, right and wrong are not based solely on legal or illegal. Just because something is legal does not make it moral. One can follow laws and still act without integrity.

I presented these five definitions in this order for a reason. Values and principles are about your beliefs and what is important to you. The actions of the Cobra Kai group provide an example of values and principles devoid of morals and integrity. Yet, in the series, people referred to the head of the Cobra Kai as their leader.

In chapter four, we addressed titles. A sensei teaches students. The word sensei is a term of honor that literally translates to "teacher." It is an honor to help others learn because a sensei teaches students to be disciplined, accountable, and act with integrity. Forms of martial arts are not about how to hit people. The students are gaining wisdom on how to have discipline in their lives—a worthy ideal.

When a sensei acts with integrity, he or she is acting in leadership, thereby, a leader at that time. Or they can be a sensei who does not act in leadership. That's how easy it is to determine when a person is or is not a leader at any moment. A position, title, or placement in any hierarchy is entirely separate from leadership.

If you were to start from scratch to define leadership, would "unethical leadership" be a label? Of course not. Would "merciless leadership" be a label? Of course not. Attaching leadership to a position in a hierarchy led to hundreds and hundreds of definitions of leadership, many of which should have been something other than a type of leadership. How about the stories of Madoff, Jones, and Delvey at the beginning of this book? What kind of leadership do those stories depict?

In his book, *There is No Such Thing as Business Ethics* (2003), John Maxwell walks us through the illusion that ethics can and should be different in business. I love how John's book begins. A prominent CEO asks John what he thinks about authoring a book on business ethics. John, without hesitation, tells him, "There's no such thing." When the CEO asks him to explain, John replies, "There's no such thing as business ethics. There's only ethics." Hence, there is no such thing as business leadership. There is only leadership. Anything devoid of integrity is not leadership, whether in business or life.

As we move from component to component within the BASIC leadership platform, we always pass through the integrity hub. Without first passing through the integrity hub, no path exists from one element to another. If a person acts unethically, then the integrity hub is the failsafe for whether that person is acting in leadership. A CEO, other executives, a senator, or a governor can act unethically, but they are in no way acting in leadership when doing so. There is no such thing as unethical leadership, only unethical, dishonest, corrupt, evil, and unscrupulous people.

As the loop of optimal effectiveness illustrates, we need a method for simplifying to achieve optimal effectiveness. We can now activate the third stage in the loop of optimal effectiveness, moving toward simplification. The integrity hub will eliminate the bulk of the current leadership labels that developed because the concept of leadership was misguidedly attached to the top positions in hierarchies and associated with doing business. We're getting close. One more component exists for determining when we are acting in leadership: The Leadership Lifeline.

CHAPTER SEVEN

Leadership Lifeline

A man sitting under a tree gets bonked in the head with an apple, and now we have orbiting space satellites. Partly true. Isaac Newton watched an apple fall, but one never hit him on the noggin. Sir Isaac Newton, an English mathematician, physicist, and astronomer, lived when the amount of information available to people would be a drop of water in a fifty-five-gallon barrel compared to what is known today. Newton lived from 1643 to 1727. His insights are legendary. Newton showed us that for every action, there is an equal and opposite reaction.

Not long after Newton had left this world, Benjamin Franklin worked diligently to understand and harness the power of electricity. Historical accounts tell us it was around 1752. Teachers worldwide use the story of Franklin flying a kite during thunderstorms. An activity not recommended today because we have more insight into the dangers. Electricity cannot exist without a positive side and a negative side. Would you want to throw out the negative side of electricity? Of course not. And if you tried, you'd fail because it's a built-in component of nature and the universe. There must be an equal and opposite reaction to everything. Positive cannot exist without negative. Good cannot exist without evil. It's not that we want evil; without it, there would be nothing to contrast against to define what good means.

Negative is normal. It's part of life. We must learn to handle the negative. Don't ignore it. Handle it. We don't have to live in it, and we don't have to dwell on it, but we do have to handle it. We handled it when we discussed the negative impacts of the word "failure" while defining success. A gardener pays attention to the weeds in their garden. They know the weeds will come. They will have to deal with them, or those weeds will take over. Our lives are our garden, and we get to handle the weeds that infest it.

Nature, in so many ways, helps us to define leadership. Nature and the universe show us the way. The minute we are all born, life thrusts us into a battle between good and evil, darkness and light, between negative and positive, between Tierney and Democracy. We are in that war, like it or not. The draft is automatic. No one is exempt. When goodness sleeps, guess who never sleeps? Evil. In the absence of light, darkness prevails. Guess who moves in if goodness does not arouse itself and become active? Evil. Positive and negative are organic. They exist naturally in our lives, in the universe.

Newton understood that for every action, there is an equal and opposite reaction. We must take action and gain insight from those actions to move toward the worthy ideal of living on the positive side of the leadership lifeline. The universe's natural order tells us that the integrity hub filter by itself, while capable of moving us down the simplicity curve, is not enough.

Many things can pass through the integrity filter because they do not violate acting with integrity, yet those things should not be any type of leadership. For example, eating too much and not exercising, which leads to being unhealthy, end up in long, drawn-out debates concerning right or wrong. A sumo wrestler needs to be significantly overweight to compete in that sport. Applying how a sumo wrestler eats to the integrity hub as a test of acting in leadership would not be effective. Beyond the integrity hub, how could we continue to answer the question, when is a person acting in leadership? The answer; The Leadership Lifeline.

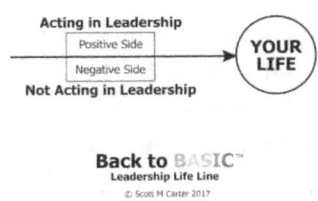

Before beginning my three-year leadership research journey, I had read a fair amount of personal development books. That is how I discovered the seventh component of the BASIC platform. The leadership lifeline was born out of the same premise Jeff Olson presents in his book *The Slight Edge*, published in 2005. Olson shows how we are constantly moving forward on a timeline. And as we progress along in time, we are never neutral in anything. During our forward progression in life, we are on one side or the other on a horizontal line. The top side of the slight edge line contains attributes such as responsibility and discipline, while the bottom side of the slight edge line contains the counterparts of those two attributes.

In this case, blame and neglect are the counterparts of responsibility and discipline. One side is positive, and the other is negative. Like the forces of gravity appeared to Newton, the idea occurred to me that any actions on the top side were actions of a leader, thereby determining when a person is acting in leadership. Using Olson's premise, the leadership lifeline allows us to go beyond the integrity hub to continue to determine when a person is acting in leadership.

Leadership is an art, not a science. People have been trying to force a scientific formula like the gravitational acceleration constant of g = 9.81 m/s2. Acting in leadership is fluid, moving in many directions while attempting to remain on the positive side of the leadership lifeline.

In his book, *Concept of the Corporation*, published in 1946, Peter Drucker provides some insight regarding leadership. He says institutions must bring out the good qualities and neutralize or deflect the bad qualities to create leaders. And that they must induce moral growth in their organizational members. Of course, he refers to leadership in a positional capacity, meaning leaders exist at the top. Yet, the qualities he describes are defined by the three stages of the BASIC Leadership platform, the outer wheel spelling out the word BASIC, the integrity hub, and the leadership lifeline.

We'll notice the combination of the three parts' overall simplicity. A person could explain all the components in three of the shortest chapters you're likely to ever see in a leadership book. And if combined into one chapter, they would still be more straightforward than most individual chapters of other books about leadership.

> *If you can't explain it simply, you don't understand it well enough.* ~Albert Einstein

When combined, the three parts allow us to effectively move a substantial distance along the third stage of the loop of optimal effectiveness. As we move forward on our leadership journey here, we'll put some things to the test so everyone can learn how the process works. And then, as the reader, you can take anything you wish and apply it to the BASIC Leadership platform yourself and see if you agree that this platform works for almost anything you throw at it.

As we test this platform together, you and I and other readers will act, gain insight, collaborate, impact our beliefs, and move toward a worthy ideal. That worthy ideal is "defining when a person is acting in leadership." During this journey, we will act with integrity, noting that the worthy ideal and our actions fall on the positive side of the leadership lifeline. We notice that we will be acting in leadership and thereby be leaders. And none of it requires a person to be in a specific position in any hierarchy. If you missed it, testing the platform against the platform meets all the criteria. We have already begun to test it.

Next, nature provides us with a great deal of insight regarding acting in leadership.

CHAPTER EIGHT

We All Have a Drug Dealer

You are out for a walk on a calm and cool night. A shadowy figure suddenly appears wearing a long overcoat, the kind gun slingers sported as part of their wardrobe in the wild west. The dark, undiscernible figure slowly opens one side of their long garment and, in a gentle, calming voice, asks, "Hey man, want some serotonin? How about some dopamine or oxytocin? I have them all."

Think you have never had a relationship with a drug dealer? *Think again.* Nature created a pharmacy in our bodies—nature, your drug dealer. The difference between nature and the bad elements selling drugs on our streets is that we cannot walk away from nature. Our bodies pump chemicals into our systems every single day. Designed to show us what acting in leadership means in its true essence, those chemicals have both positive and negative effects.

If you were asked what chemicals nature has put into our little personal pharmacies, could you name any if I hadn't given you three in the opening paragraph? And just as important, what causes each one to be released, and what effect it has on you? Again, don't feel bad; most people cannot.

Our actions and the actions of others cause the release of a multitude of chemicals into our bodies. We will gain insight into six natural chemicals: endorphins, dopamine, serotonin, oxytocin, cortisol, and adrenaline. The big mac daddy of all questions is, *why do these chemicals exist in the first place?* The answer? Nature helps us define when we are acting in leadership.

Cortisol.

Cortisol, the primary stress hormone, increases sugars (glucose) in the bloodstream, enhances your brain's use of glucose and increases the availability of substances that repair tissues. I don't know about you, but I want my body to be able to repair tissue. We need cortisol. However, there is always a yin and yang, a balance to life. Stress and anxiety release cortisol. Guess what happens if a person is always stressed out or anxious? Nature punishes us. Excessive amounts of this chemical damage our cells and can lead to things like cancer. That's a pretty darn good reason to pay attention to stress and anxiety.

Our drug dealer, nature, may not ask for money when it divvies out cortisol, but there is always a price to pay. I find it fascinating how those who hold top-level positions in organizations assume that when a person is not stressed or anxious about missing a random arbitrary monetary goal, they think that person does not care. Somehow we equate stress and anxiety with caring, and even worse, we equate it with being a leader. Yet, what do we say that leaders do? They remain calm. Who should remain calm? All of us. Why? Because the chemical drip, drip, drip of cortisol from stress can kill us very slowly.

Society teaches us stress. It is a learned behavior. And we do it to ourselves. We add activity after activity to our plates. The kids need to be in three sports. We need to work late and impress the boss. We need a huge house and a plethora of gadgets and toys, all of which require maintenance and take up space somewhere. I bought some new things, and I rarely use them because I don't have the time. Sounds silly, right? But that's what we do, and it all creates stress. Drip, drip, drip, the cortisol enters our bodies.

During my career, I have held the top position in different departments. In the latter part of my career, I frequently heard statements like, "You're always so calm no matter what happens." That wasn't always the case. I was a hothead when I was young. The smallest of things would set me off. I'd get mad at objects like the object did something to me and was at fault. I remember trying to attach a backrest and luggage carrier to my first motorcycle. When I struggled, I blew up, cursing the bike and the backrest, blaming those inanimate objects. And, of course, looking to the sky and blaming God.

Looking back, I often wondered what the neighbors thought of how I acted. Now I choose to be calm, not to release cortisol into my body. Not only was the stress self-induced, but I also combined it with anger, releasing another chemical, adrenaline.

Adrenaline

Adrenaline is responsible for your body's 'fight or flight' response. It helps you react quickly in a dangerous or stressful situation. Adrenaline is released when your brain perceives excitement, danger, fear, or a potential threat. We use the phrase "adrenaline junkie" to describe thrill seekers who jump out of planes and free fall before opening their parachutes. We should know nature provides a pharmacy in our bodies because we talk about being junkies.

If your adrenal glands produce too much adrenaline, it can cause high blood pressure from pheochromocytoma. There's a ten-dollar word. We can get bad headaches and high blood pressure from too much adrenaline, yet some self-induce through thrill-seeking. Adrenaline's true purpose is to keep us alive, to give us short bursts of extraordinary strength and energy for self-preservation. When we get angry, we release adrenaline, which should be reserved for self-preservation. Now I choose not to get angry, to not self-induce with adrenaline. We self-induce with other chemicals as well.

Dopamine

Dopamine is both a self-preservation and a reward chemical. Nature has created a "feel good" chemical that rewards us for setting and accomplishing goals. When you accomplish something such as planting and harvesting food, the result of completing that goal and all the little successes along the way give us a shot of dopamine. Drip, drip, drip, yum, yum. In other words, taking action toward a worthy ideal where we experience success gets rewarded. That's pretty cool, folks. And, as always, too much of a good thing can be harmful.

Too much of this feel-good hormone can lead to negative behaviors like overly competitive, aggressive, or having poor impulse control. Some people become addicted to eating, gambling, sex, drinking, or recreational drugs. Yes, even man-made drugs release drugs from nature's internal pharmacy.

Eat a yummy, not-so-good-for-you snack, then drip, drip, drip, you get some dopamine. Gamble and win, then drip, drip. I do it with my grocery lists. When I go to the store and find something I forgot to put on my list, I grab the item off the shelf, then write it on the list and cross it off. Drip, drip, give me some more of that. It's good stuff.

We get addicted to the little doses of dopamine that technology can create. People post something on a social media platform or send ten people a text, then wait for a like, comment, or response. The little beeps and dings of the text messages and notifications on our cell phones cause the drip, drip, drip of dopamine into our bodies. We get addicted to the sounds our phones make. It's like we're out for Halloween and tricking people into giving us more candy. "Hey, look, I'm a pirate. Put some candy in my sack. Hey, I posted a selfie. Give me a shot of dopamine."

Nature designed dopamine as a reward to ensure we were motivated to survive. Surviving a day or week in modern times is not a real issue. Food is abundant and easily accessible except in third-world countries. We're not being chased by large animals or trying to hunt big game for their meat and skins. Technology and an abundance of food in most countries do not require a lot of survival skills. Instead, not acting in leadership is constantly dripping oxytocin into our bodies, which is harmful. We're tricking nature into giving us more drugs, like writing an illegal prescription at our local pharmacy, except our bodies have no law against doing so. Negative behaviors like being overly competitive, aggressive, or having poor impulse control work against acting in leadership.

Endorphins

Endorphins mask pain. Over the millennia, our bodies have developed many ways to help us survive. For a very long time, life was different than it is now, requiring hunting and gathering, long journeys, and abundant hardships. Nature knew this. During these challenging times, a hunter or traveler might be injured. Nature said, "Hey, I can help you to continue with less pain." Endorphin comes from the words "endogenous," which means within the body, and "morphine," an opiate pain reliever. Endorphins are a feel-good chemical because they can make us feel better and put us in a positive state of mind.

Our body releases endorphins when it feels pain and when we are stressed. Yay! Nature is helping us to counter that awful stress. We also get a shot of this good stuff during pleasurable activities such as exercise, massages, eating, and sex. The last one helps us to see why endorphins fit the self-preservation category. Sex leads to procreation, the continuation of our species.

Endorphins do not play as crucial a role as cortisol or dopamine, so why include it? Because, it illustrates just how thorough nature has been when it comes to creating pharmacies in our bodies. Nature is so smart that is also gave us two collaboration chemicals.

Oxytocin

Our body releases oxytocin during childbirth and lactation to feed the newborn. Oxytocin also acts as a chemical messenger in your brain and plays a vital role in human behaviors. The first is the parent-infant bonding. Others include social interactions such as sexual arousal, recognition, trust, and romantic attachment.

Oxytocin is a chemical that provides the feeling we get from emotional bonds and physical touch. It's a collaboration chemical designed to reward us for the right behaviors. This is why all the separation, social distancing, lockdowns, and masking during covid have had such negative effects on society, leading to a rise in depression and suicidal attempts.

Oxytocin builds up slowly and stays in the system longer than adrenaline or dopamine. You can't get addicted to oxytocin. When we have oxytocin in our bodies, it reduces our susceptibility to things that do cause addiction. For example, we can counter the addictive chemical dopamine. Because oxytocin builds up slowly, we say, "Trust takes time." We judge each other by the consistency of our behaviors, not just one or two events. Over time we decide if we trust someone.

Whether at work or in our personal lives, when a person violates the integrity hub and acts or thinks on the negative side of the leadership lifeline, then there is no oxytocin for anyone. We can kiss collaboration goodbye. This aspect of life is so important that nature doubled up on it.

Serotonin

Serotonin plays several roles in our bodies, including influencing learning, memory, and happiness, as well as regulating body temperature, sleep, sexual behaviors, and hunger. Fairly significant, wouldn't you agree?

When someone else's actions make us feel the emotion of pride, that is because of the chemical serotonin. It's ok to feel pride, but not ok to be prideful. There is a difference. Serotonin boosts our confidence and makes us feel fantastic. Why is public recognition so powerful? We get a shot of serotonin, those doing the recognition get a shot of serotonin, and those seeing the recognition also get a shot of this beautiful chemical. That's how nature approached collaboration. Giving credit to others and sharing the credit with others creates a bond between people.

Nature. More intelligent than all of us.

What do you get when you cross a hunting dog with a telephone? A Golden Receiver. What do you get when you cross a chicken with a centipede? Enough drumsticks to feed an army. What do you get when you combine an elephant and a rhino? Elephino (El-if-I-know). That last one is what most people would say when you ask what chemicals nature provides in our bodies and why. Yeah, cheesy dad jokes. Suck it up, buttercup.

Dopamine has been linked to intrinsic motivation in goal accomplishment, whether academic, personal, or professional. Oxytocin is a collaboration chemical designed to reward us for the right behaviors. We get a shot of serotonin for giving recognition, and those who witness that act also get a dose. We also get punished chemically for not acting in leadership. Stress and anger, mostly self-induced, can take years off of our lives.

All of these are leadership chemicals. During my research I have found a pattern associated with calling one of these six "the leadership" chemical. This was born out of associating leadership with a position in organizational hierarchies and doing business.

Nature did not say, "I will reward you for influencing others, inspiring others, or acquiring followers." Nature is more innovative than all of us combined regarding leadership, including our ability to distinguish between a worthy ideal and forms of escalation. Let's address those things next, as well as what we think we require to be content or happy.

CHAPTER NINE

Worthy Ideals, Escalation, Happiness, and Contentment

Lust, gluttony, greed, sloth, wrath, envy, and pride. Nope, those do not make up *The Bill of Rights*. The way some people act, one might come to that conclusion in today's society. They are the seven deadly sins.

Would these seven items pass through the integrity hub? On which side of the leadership lifeline would those attributes land? When a person reads about this list of seven behaviors, the incorrect story is that they came from the *Bible*. The *Bible* validates them, but nowhere are they recorded in a list like this, and nowhere in the *Bible* are they specifically referred to as the seven deadly sins. Pope Gregory I compiled this list around the year 600 AD. Gregory also put together a list of the seven virtues: faith, hope, charity, justice, prudence, temperance, and fortitude, giving balance to the seven sins. A yin and yang exist for everything.

Regardless of who created those lists, intrinsically, we know which side of the leadership lifeline both lists exist. We do not have to think twice or have long, drawn-out debates. But what about a worthy ideal? Can we make the same determination about what constitutes a worthy ideal when someone presents one to us?

A man or woman decides to stay home and raise their children rather than build a career while putting their children in daycare. Is that a worthy ideal? Yes. I have yet to find a person who says no to that question. How about starting and growing a business? Sure it is. If you hesitated in answering that question, why did you? Because, up until now, we confused leadership with doing business.

We learned how the BASIC Leadership platform defines when a person acts in leadership. We then wondered if business itself has anything to do with leadership. It does not. It's just business, just as raising children is just parenting. Acting in leadership is defined by our behaviors while progressing toward a worthy ideal. Creating a business, growing it, and providing jobs because we live in a monetary society could be deemed a worthy ideal, but having a worthy ideal does not automatically translate to acting in leadership.

We confuse success with materialistic wants and the accumulation of wealth. We then compare ourselves to others to determine if we are successful. Tom and Beth have college degrees. They make a lot of money, have a nice home, and have two new cars. Ahhhh, success. Shaniqua and Tyrell own their own business. They have four stores, excellent customer reviews on Google, and travel to Italy to look for new products to sell. Their search for new products allows them to experience other parts of the world. Ahhhh, success.

Is the following a business objective or worthy ideal? "We want to become the fastest-growing company with the highest profit margins in the business of renting and leasing vehicles without drivers." Know who came up with that? Avis car rental under Robert Townsend's guidance while competing against Hertz. What does Townsend call it in his book? A business objective.

We have experts telling us that growth for the sake of growth is a bad business platform—gluttony and greed. They also tell us that hubris is the downfall of many organizations—excessive pride or self-confidence. Yet, when we talk about business and organizations, we call those acting with hubris and pushing growth for the sake of growth leaders and part of leadership teams. Then we wonder why people are confused about the concept of leadership.

We can quickly see how this ties into the pharmacies that nature put into our bodies. Did the little light bulb go on over your head? Did you just have an "ah ha" moment?

Do not compare, do not measure. No other way is like yours. All other ways deceive you and tempt you. You must fulfill the way that is in you. ~Carl Jung

Contentment, Happiness, and Escalation

We live in a society of perpetual escalation. Power, wealth, material possessions, bigger, better, and all that big and better implies are depictions of perpetual escalation.

Did you realize that we confuse achieving contentment and happiness with escalation? The states of happiness and contentment can only exist in the present. Nothing exists in the future except the unknown. We tend to look to the future for happiness and contentment through unknown perpetual escalation of some arbitrary number, position, or status, with the intent of increasing power, wealth, and material possessions, and more of bigger and better. Bigger and more are not the progression of a worthy ideal but perpetual escalation.

Then we achieve that arbitrary number, position, or status only to find out that happiness and contentment if they come at all, are momentary. Then what? More of the same? More growth, an increase, a heightening, or a widening; call it what you will. And all for what? For something that was already yours. Let me repeat that, *for something that was already yours—Happiness and contentment.*

> *Remember, happiness doesn't depend upon who you are or what you have; it depends solely upon what you think. ~Dale Carnegie*

When you reach that future, will you be content? Or will you postpone contentment for some other future?

Once we see that question, we understand that any escalation is actually a roadblock to contentment and happiness. Why? Because you do not need those things to be in a state of happiness and contentment. You can possess happiness and contentment without any escalation. The constant drive for more and more and more is an invention, and even worse, a myth that somehow ongoing escalation will create contentment and happiness.

> *You cannot become happy with what you might obtain in the future – not until that future becomes the present.* ~Dr. Laurence J. Peter

What does this have to do with leadership? Someone will inevitably try to tie escalation into the "Success" component of the BASIC Leadership platform. Our definition of success is "the progressive realization of a worthy ideal." Progression, often confused with escalation, is different than escalation. Look up synonyms for escalate and progress. Progressive realization is not an escalation. Tying escalation to leadership occurred when we equated leadership with doing business and a position in a hierarchy. One can act in leadership while doing business, but business has nothing to do with leadership. Likewise, a person can have a worthy ideal, but that does not equate to acting in leadership.

Lots of people are "doing life" and "doing parenting," and most of us are "doing business." Still, the worthy ideal itself does not mean a person is acting in leadership and being a leader, nor is escalation the same as progression. We can do a lot of things without acting in leadership. In most cases, we're just doing business.

CHAPTER TEN

It's Just Business

It's the mid-1970s. Steve Jobs was a video game designer and had just returned from a pilgrimage to India to experience Buddhism. That autumn Steve Jobs reconnects with Stephen Wozniak, a former high school friend. Wozniak tells Jobs of his progress in designing his computer logic board. Two years later, Hewlett Packard, yes, that same company most of us know as HP, turns down Wozniak's design. At that point, Wozniak and Jobs began building the Apple I logic board in Jobs' family garage. They used the money they obtained by selling Jobs' Volkswagen minibus and Wozniak's programmable calculator.

Whether you know the story of Apple, Wozniak, and Jobs, or have never heard how Apple began, I have a couple of questions for you. When would you say that they became leaders? And when did they start acting in leadership? And tell us why. In other words, provide your premise for when and how.

The famous computer duo had a worthy ideal. Wozniak and Jobs believed in that worthy ideal and acted on it, and through those actions, they progressed toward it. Sometimes they had successes. Sometimes they did not. Through both the nonsuccesses and the successes, they gained insight. When they acted with integrity, and their actions landed on the positive side of the leadership lifeline, they were acting in leadership, thereby a leader at any given moment.

They also acted out of leadership and were not leaders at any given moment when they violated the integrity hub test and landed on the negative side of the leadership lifeline. We all move in and out of acting in leadership. We move in and out of being leaders. Now it's your turn. Tell us when they acted in leadership, and when they became leaders.

There is a distinction between acting in leadership and doing business. In 1999 Jack Welch of GE was named "Manager of the Century." Notice the award providers didn't give Welch the label of "Leader of the Century." That's because the designation of manager was given in relation to doing business. Over the years, Welch laid people off to increase the company's bottom line. And he did it while the organization was profitable, not because the company would go under due to lack of profit. Welch was doing business, which had little to do with acting in leadership. It's just business. I'm not implying that saying "it's just business" makes any negative behavior or lack of integrity acceptable. It means that those actions do not deserve any leadership label. In its true essence, leadership has nothing to do with business except that anyone, regardless of their status in an organizational hierarchy, can act in leadership while doing business.

In its true essence, leadership has nothing to do with business except that anyone, regardless of their status in an organizational hierarchy, can act in leadership while doing business. ~Scott M. Carter

Inherently, we know that leadership is not a position in any hierarchy. It cannot be, or the only way a person can be a leader and attain leadership is by climbing an organizational chart. Associating leadership with doing business is in direct contrast to the natural order of life. We want everyone to act like leaders, then tell people they are not leaders until they get a position of authority in some hierarchy. Then when that person arrives at or near the top, and they lack integrity, we say we have a leadership problem. No, we have an unethical CEO, unethical executive, or unethical politician problem.

Attaching the concepts of leader and leadership to a position in a hierarchy and primarily associating it with doing business allowed us to create a massive number of labels. Leadership in its purest form does not allow such labels to exist. What we want is for people to act in leadership while doing business. What has been missing up to this point is defining when a person is acting in leadership. Now we have the formula.

Business Management vs. Leadership

Those who study leadership and business management are familiar with Peter Drucker. He was mentioned in an earlier chapter. For those unfamiliar with Peter Drucker, Drucker is known as the father of modern management. He has written over 30 books, beginning with his first in 1939. Not one of his book titles contains the words leader or leadership. *Wait! What?*

Peter Drucker wrote about organizations, their function, and business strategies, not leadership. Drucker tells us so in his book *Management Challenges for the 21st Century*, published in 1999. Right at the very beginning of this book, he makes it clear that the book is not about leadership. Perhaps he grew tired of people equating business with leadership, and subconsciously he understood the two are distinctly different. That leadership wasn't a position in a hierarchy, but that's a guess on my part. I have a question for all the business majors who have studied Drucker. Yes, he referred to people at the top of the hierarchy as leaders, but why, if Drucker does not equate business activities with leadership, are we still attaching leadership to a position in a hierarchy? Perhaps a good thesis paper for your master's degree.

For those familiar with Jim Collins, you'll quickly recognize his business books. Collins wrote *Built to Last* (1994), *Good To Great* (2001), and *How The Mighty Fall* (2009). That's right. First, we learned how companies were built to last. Then Collins lays out a formula for how they went from good to great. Apparently, that's how they ended up built to last. But then some of them fell. If you have a comical grin on your face right now, it's ok. Most people do after reading that. His entire series of books address the longevity of organizations. I argue that Collins did not write about what constitutes leadership. He wrote about the business decisions that CEOs and other executives made during their tenure with those companies. Let me ask you another question. Do you think a company that produces a product known to shorten the lives of people who use the product is great?

> "Warning: The Surgeon General has determined that cigarette smoking is dangerous to your health."

Collins uses a method that compares two companies in the same industry to show which one is good or not so good and which one became great. Phillip Morris and R.J. Reynolds are two of those companies. Both produce products with that Surgeon General warning on the packaging. It is not illegal to produce those products or to purchase those products if you are 18 or older. People buy them of their own free will, at least at first. Acting within the legal limits of a society is not the same as acting with integrity. It's just business. I love Collin's work. He has great insight on what creates longevity in organizations. Want to create longevity in your organization? Gain some insight from his works.

All books that illustrate studies of organizations tell us about business strategies and plans implemented or not implemented that either helped or hindered the growth of an organization. All those stories about these entities illustrate hindsight of past decisions, and none provide us with any organization's future strategy or plan. They did not write about leadership; they wrote about past business decisions. A company that produces cigarettes does not have a leadership team; they have an executive team making business decisions.

It's 1992, two years before Collins publishes his book *Built to Last*. Can you tell me the name of the book that Jack Stack and Bo Burlington published that year? The answer is, *The Great Game of Business: The Only Sensible Way to Run a Company.*

In 1983 International Harvester was taking steps to shut down one of its plants. This particular plant produced rebuilt engine blocks. Jack Stack and eleven other managers scraped together $100,000, borrowed $8.9 million, and bought that dying division of International Harvester. Together, they transformed it into what has become SRC Holdings.

When I say "transformed," I mean a company that other organizations travel across the globe to visit and participate in what they call the Gathering of Games. How many people and companies travel to participate? By the 20th anniversary of the Gathering of Games event in 2012, fifteen thousand people from five thousand companies had already done so. Why?

We love business numbers, don't we? In 2013 an updated version of the book, *The Great Game of Business*, was released. Jack Stack gives us some comparisons to show how SRC has performed. He frames it this way. If you had invested $1,000 in a Standard's and Poor's index fund in 1983 when SRC began, that investment would be worth $8,434. If you had invested that same $1,000 into Berkshire Hathaway, Warren Buffet's company, over the same time frame, your stake in that company would be worth about $113,000. Take the same $1,000; had you invested it in the people of SRC in 1984, you'd be worth $3.4 million in 2013.

How often have you heard people reference Warren Buffet, Peter Drucker, or the companies Jim Collins talks about in his books? If you're in business and a student of learning, the answer is *a lot*. Here's the point of all these numbers and references. In that same introduction, in the updated version of *The Great Game of Business*, Jack Stack tells us, "it's business." At SRC, they teach everyone from top to bottom how to run a business. Most companies teach people how to "build their product or service," but rarely do people learn how to "build a business." So SRC began to teach people at all levels how to build and run a company. When Stack does talk about leadership, it applies to everyone. Stack refers to the Great Game of Business, GGOB, as a leadership system and tells us it has nothing to do with the organization's hierarchy.

Stories of companies like SRC would not make it into any of the books written by Collins, or many other business books, because SRC didn't meet the study criteria. SRC was too small and not in business long enough. Whether you agree with what Stack and

Burlington tell us or what Collins tells us, business is the subject they address. For SRC, leadership is not a position in their hierarchy. SRC understood the distinction between leadership and doing business. The financial comparisons you read above are a result of getting it right. We apply random labels to lots of things. Would you like some almond milk?

CHAPTER ELEVEN

Families, Root Causes, and Milk

Honey, We Have to Fire One of the Kids!

We get so many things wrong. When did people attempt to link a business with a family? Sure, there are family businesses, meaning businesses privately owned by a family. What if you run your family like a business? What would that look like?

You're married, and you have three children. You're at home, just finished your annual budget, and are admiring your financial accomplishments for the year. You had a goal of saving a certain amount of money for retirement, building college funds for all three kids, and the usual laundry list of things we look at financially. The numbers show that you did not reach your goal for your projected retirement or the plan for all three kid's college funds. You've come up short. The family made a profit, and there is plenty of money, so you're a profitable family. You are much better off than the previous year. However, you didn't reach your goals. If you can manipulate the numbers to show you have reached your financial goals, the family stock will go up. That's always an option since that's what many companies do. It's decision time. After all, mom and dad are stakeholders, and they have expectations for profitability and growth. Which kid gets laid off? One must be let go.

Sounds absurd? That's what Jack Welch did at GE. Why are we trying to say organizations are families? Your company isn't a family. Pretending otherwise is unhealthy and unproductive. Families don't fire people. I bet you've disappointed your mother countless times – I know I did. Mom never fired me for poor performance and didn't lay me off when quarterly projections didn't hit the target metrics. Basing family loyalty on performance or profitability would be absurd.

I've worked for two large stock-held corporations and three privately owned companies. The transitions in my career from one company to another happened because of "it's just business" circumstances. One company was purchased by another company, and then my position was eliminated. In another case, a company purchased the company where I worked and then shut down the entire company. Why? Because the acquiring company bought it for the territory distribution rights to expand its footprint.

I'm glad these transitions happened. I acquired a boatload of business experience. Is there anything unethical about companies doing any of these things? How about immoral? In the case where the company was acquired, part of the agreement of the acquisition was that actual family members were guaranteed jobs in the acquiring company. The rest of us? Just employees. Unless your parents or a direct family member owns the company where you work, you are an employee.

You see, it's just business. Calling your business a family is an internal organizational marketing tactic done to create the feeling of absolute loyalty toward the company. You must love and care for your company – whatever it takes – in any circumstances. Your business is not a family, it's a business, and there are consequences for acting under the false family premise.

Who knows where this metaphor started, but referring to your business as some type of "family" has unintended consequences. Work-life boundaries can get blurred, dedicated employees can be taken advantage of, and an employee looking to leave an organization can be seen as a betrayal.

Imagine you have reached adulthood, found the love of your life, you get married, move to another city, and start your own family. Would this be a betrayal to your family consisting of your parents and siblings? The effects of calling your business a family is creating pushback among employees.

Saying leadership is a position in an organization and associating leadership with doing business have equally harmful effects. Referring to a company, organization, team, or department as a family creates issues. We are quickly realizing this mistake. Likewise, saying leadership is a position in any hierarchy has created problems, and this took a much longer time to recognize. For over 90 years, we have been misguided in attaching the concept of leadership to a position in organizational hierarchies and associating it with doing business. This entire book illustrates all the issues associated with how we've mishandled the concept of leadership. The biggest issue? Less people are acting in leadership than ever before. Rather than address the root cause, we treat symptoms.

Root Cause Versus Treating the Symptoms

We live in a world where the standard, it appears, has become treating symptoms rather than addressing the root cause. A symptom is something that happens as a result of the root cause of a problem.

According to the Center for Disease Control, CDC, heart disease is the leading cause of death in the United States. If I asked you to name just three of the top five primary reasons, could you? Unhealthy diet, physical inactivity, and stress. Those are the root causes.

Now I'll ask you the obvious question. Do most people address the root causes, or do they treat the symptoms?

We do not act in leadership by eating healthily and exercising, which address some of the root causes. Then, after the damage is done, we want to treat the symptoms of obesity through medication, surgery, or other methods.

When you try to buy something on credit, and then your purchase is denied, the denial might be a symptom of having bad credit. The root cause is that you didn't act in leadership by maintaining good credit by living on the positive side of the leadership lifeline. Now you have to try to repair your credit, which is treating the symptom.

When you lack motivation, whose job is it to get you motivated? It's yours. Burnout, stress, and boredom are some root causes of lack of motivation. Rather than develop the mindset that motivation is your responsibility, we place the responsibility of motivation onto someone else. That someone else is generally located in a position somewhere higher up in an organizational chart. For example, when a front line worker is not motivated, the manager is now said to be responsible for motivating that person.

When we refer to the person higher up the organizational chart as a leader, and make motivating others one of their objectives, the term "motivational leadership" is created to describe that new responsibility.

The root cause is that the person lacking the motivation has not gained the insight to understand that motivating yourself is how a person acts in leadership. Teaching everyone, from a very early age that acting in leadership requires you to be motivated all on your own addresses the root cause—Just as eating healthy and exercising addresses the root causes of heart disease.

Calling your company a family is a version of treating the symptoms and not addressing the root cause of why people are disengaged at work.

An Almond Milking Plant

If I asked you, "Where does milk come from? What constitutes milk?" How would you answer? It's a fluid secreted through a female mammal's breast to nourish its young. That process is called lactation and creates milk. Yet we now have almond milk. Why? Because taking a liquid made from almonds sells better when we call it milk. An almond cannot lactate. Cows can lactate. Therefore, we have cow's milk. Almond milk sounds better than almond juice. It's marketing. It's business.

Taking an adjective and placing it in front of the word leadership does not make that a type of leadership, just like placing the word milk after the word almond does not magically turn a liquid produced from almonds into a kind of milk. Are you ready for the nutty part? (Pun intended). This marketing ploy of labeling almonds as milk has become a legal battle. Why? Because it's just business.

If milk comes from mammals and not nuts, then where does leadership come from, if not the top of hierarchies? The history of the word itself can provide some insight.

CHAPTER TWELVE

History of Leadership

> Presentism: uncritical adherence to present-day attitudes, especially the tendency to interpret past events in terms of modern values and concepts.

That's the dictionary definition. In simple terms, it means judging everyone in the past by current standards. It's the belief that people who lived a hundred, five hundred, or a thousand years ago should have known better. It's like getting mad at yourself for not knowing what you know now when you were ten or twelve years old.

Silly me, spending all that time raising sea monkeys or collecting pet rocks. Who hasn't said, "I can't believe I said that." Or "I can't believe I used to believe that." I smoked and was into astrology. I do not look back and say, "I should have known better." I say, "I have so much more insight now."

The journey of life, for all eternity, has been and is the process of taking action, gaining insight, establishing and changing beliefs, moving toward worthy ideals, and collaborating. We cannot apply today's knowledge and events to the past to say that others should have gotten it right. That's not how it works, or your stupid ten-year-old self would have never done all those things you now look back at and either laugh or cringe.

They should have known the earth was round. Not really. Although I would argue that they should have known the earth wasn't flat. Because if it were, cats would have pushed everything off the edge within a year. If you're interested in becoming a member of the Flat Earther Society, people from all around the globe can join. "Around the globe" is actually used in their messaging.

They should have known that the sun didn't revolve around the earth, and they should have known that leadership was not a position in any hierarchy are bad arguments to make. Instead, we now have the insight to take action and correct how leadership was misguidedly associated with business and attached a position in hierarchies. We know better.

For instance, in his book *On Becoming a Leader*, published in 1989, Warren Bennis says, "Managers are people who do things right, and leaders are people who do the right thing." That means that whoever is at the top of a hierarchy, whether the Board of Directors, CEO, or other Executives, darn well better be good at making high-level business decisions, or the ship will sink, or as

Jim Collins says, the mighty will fall. And those under them in the hierarchy need to be proficient at the tasks required to keep the business bus rolling toward the decision the executive makes. That's how business works.

Instead, Bennis talks about how leaders make leadership decisions regarding the direction of an organization and that managers follow the processes. CEOs or Boards of Directors make business decisions and have little to do with being a leader other than, at times, they might act in leadership while doing business.

In chapter four of this book, the one you are reading right now, there was a fill-in-the-blank exercise. Most people insert CEO or another executive title to define who is responsible for the duties listed. Here is where the wires became crossed regarding business and leadership. Starting in the early 1900s, while people were trying to define and develop theories regarding leadership, business practices were changing. Let me repeat that. *Business practices were changing.* There was a huge focus on the duties and responsibilities of those who held the highest positions in the hierarchies.

Those who studied and wrote about business were trying to answer a couple of fundamental questions. Were the things the CEO and other executives doing moving the organization forward in the most effective way possible? What are the responsibilities of the people at the top levels of any organization?

Look at the language in the book *Leaders* by Warren Bennis and Burt Nanus, published in 1985. Reading the entire book would be optimal, but if you're short on time, start at page 175 and read to the end. Now that I have pointed out that the book's focus is "a shift in responsibilities" and has nothing to do with leadership, it'll jump right off the pages and stomp on your foot.

The book is about the shift in responsibilities at the top of business hierarchies. You will notice this in all business books attempting to define leadership. Reading leadership books produced in the 1950s up through the 1980s can be boring for some people. Therefore, I recommend a more entertaining book.

In 1969, Dr. Laurence J. Peter and Raymond Hull, published their book, *The Peter Principle*. The book is a satirical approach to the responsibilities of positions within a hierarchy. Make sure you read the introduction by Raymond Hull. You'll quickly discover that these two guys were not a pair of stuffy suits. I bet they were a blast to hang out with and have a beer or two. Most people familiar with *The Peter Principle* run around parroting the phrase, "In a hierarchy, every employee tends to rise to his level of incompetence." The overall premise of the book goes deeper.

Peter and Hull use funny character names and fictitious company names to illustrate their findings behind the research. The way they approach writing the book reminded me of the introduction at the beginning of the tv series *Dragnet* which first appeared in 1951. The introduction to that show stated, "The story you are about to see is true. The names have been changed to protect the innocent." In the case of the book, *The Peter*

Principle, the stories you read about are true. The names have been changed to protect the incompetent.

The book does illustrate how incompetence becomes apparent as we climb hierarchies. However, Dr. Peter Laurence founded a new science he calls hierarchiology, the study of hierarchies. The book is about hierarchies. Of all the books I've read about placement within organizations, this one has provided more insight than most others combined. Want to figure out what to do, what not to do, or understand why people react the way they do to advancements within any hierarchy? Read this book. It's enlightening and humorous. The only way to guarantee you'll be at the top of any hierarchy? *Start your own.*

When people move from one position to another in any hierarchy, their responsibilities change. Incompetence indeed follows when a person does not know what they are now responsible for doing. Changing the title of a CEO or any other executive to "leader" will not fix incompetence. Understanding the responsibilities of a position within any hierarchy will minimize or reduce incompetence. Defining a more optimal list of duties for a position at the top of a hierarchy does not equate to leadership. It equates to new responsibilities.

During the many stages of the attempts to understand the concept of leadership, we experienced a transition period regarding the responsibilities of those at the top of organizational hierarchies. That's what experts and authors were illustrating to people. Here is an example of what a list of some modern-day responsibilities might look like.

> CEOs and executives must fully understand people's behavioral traits to increase innovation, long-term thinking, collaboration, and engagement, and how rewards and punishments drive behaviors.

It had nothing to do with leadership in its true essence. Bennis' 1985 book provides an example of how the label of leadership ended up as a position in a hierarchy, and people equated making high-level business decisions with acting in leadership. We know better now.

I chose Warren Bennis to make critical points about the difference between doing business and acting in leadership because Bennis was revolutionary in changing how CEOs and executives think about what they do in organizations. In 2020, we have a great deal more information available than they did, and we can use it to gain insight. Let's look at the history of leadership.

Defining a more optimal list of duties for a position at the top of a hierarchy does not equate to leadership. It equates to new responsibilities. ~Scott M. Carter

History of Leadership

- Etymology is the history of a word or word element, including its origins and derivation. Derivation is the development of something from a source or origin.

- The root word for leadership is lead from the Anglo-Saxon Old English word *loedan*, the form of lithan – *to travel*. It means to *go somewhere* or *do something first*. To lead the way does not require anyone to go with you. When we talk about the root word of lead, "traveling" means to go first. For example, the first person to challenge a concept or idea is one who went first. They traveled there. And others can travel there, also challenging that same concept or idea without being followers. Traveling goes beyond physically moving from point A to point B. Technology advancements are examples of going somewhere first. Stephen Wozniak and Steve Jobs went somewhere first regarding technology.
- The word leadership itself came into existence in the very late 1700s. It became part of the vernacular, meaning part of the spoken language, around 1828 when Webster's *An American Dictionary of the English Language* first defined leadership. This is why in early chapters I stated that leadership is an invention. Because it is.
- The suffix -ship has a long history in English, going back to Old English. In Modern English, the suffix – ship has been added only to nouns. Adding "-ship" to a word can indicate a state or condition, such as authorship,

kinship, partnership, and relationship. Or it can be a designation such as craftsmanship, horsemanship, and sportsmanship, or rank or office such as ambassadorship, kingship, and lordship.

While I dug reasonably deep into the concept of leadership during my research, others have taken it to extreme levels, like the process of painstakingly excavating five-thousand-year-old tombs in Egypt with a tweezers and a hand brush. What did they find?

On November 6-8, Guadalajara, Jalisco, Mexico, 2003, they held the annual conference of the International Leadership Association. During the conference, Miriam Grace presents the *Origins of Leadership: The Etymology of Leadership*. Grace tells us, "The attachment of -ship to the word leader is unusual in its late arrival on the etymology scene. Many similarly constructed words had fallen into disuse long before the word leadership appeared." Grace uncovered a profound historical element that provides us with some insight.

For example, we do not talk about lordships anymore, and there is a reason why we do not. If you were asked what it means to be noble, how would you define it? Being noble was attached to a position. To be noble, one had to be of a specific lineage. Being noble was a birthright. It was a societal status. One could only compete in jousting tournaments if one were of nobility. Is being noble still attached to a position in a hierarchy? The answer is no. Who can act in nobility, and who can be noble today? The answer is anyone. There are two definitions of noble.

1) belonging to a hereditary class with high social or political status; aristocratic, and

2) having or showing fine personal qualities or high moral principles and ideals.

The two distinctly different definitions must remain so we can answer three questions.

I.   Where were we, and why?
II. Where are we now, and why?
III. Where are we going, and why?

We're defining our past, present, and potential future. While I present some research in this book, the one you are reading right now, this is not a research book. In my first book, *Leadership: Achieving Optimal Effectiveness*, I provided the details of my research. This book sets the record straight - fixing the concept of leadership as we have fixed concepts such as nobility. Insight and wisdom based on the last 130 years tell us where we were, where we are now, where we want to go, and why in all three cases.

Like the concept of nobility, leadership also has two definitions.

1) the action of leading a group of people or an organization, and

2) the state or position of being a leader.

In the second definition, the words "state" and "position" do not infer a position in a hierarchy. If it does not refer to a position in a hierarchy, then what does it refer to?

The best way to describe it is to relate it to a person's character. For instance, Reverend Martin Luther King Jr. said, "I have a dream that my four little children will one day live in a nation where they will not be judged by the color of their skin, but by the content of their character."

In other words, by how they act, which when it comes to character means with integrity and on the positive side of the lifeline.

The first definition of leadership requires a person to be judged by the position they hold in a hierarchy. The second has nothing to do with any hierarchy or with doing business. The two definitions of nobility work the same way as the two definitions of leadership. The second definition of noble is about character. We no longer associate being noble with societal status but with character. We need to do the same thing with the concept of leadership. We should no longer associate leadership with a position in a hierarchy or define it through the acts of doing business.

Notice that Reverend King's dream is a worthy ideal. It is based on a set of beliefs. It requires people to take action to move toward that worthy ideal, sometimes little successes and occasionally little non-successes. Along that journey, we gain insight, and collaboration is necessary to make it happen.

Another example of the second definition of leadership is that I am taking the stance that leadership is not a position in any hierarchy and has nothing to do with business. That is my position. It is my belief. I am taking action on that position. Someone else might take the stance that leadership is a position in a hierarchy. That is their belief, and they can choose to take action based on that belief.

Both definitions of leadership exist, and it is imperative that both remain so that we understand where we were and why, where we are now and why, and where we are headed and why. While both exist, one provides a more optimal path to simplicity, allowing us to increase our effectiveness in defining when a person is acting in leadership.

We do not act rightly because we have virtue or excellence, but we rather have those because we have acted rightly. ~Plato

Plato enlightened us on virtue in the middle of fourth century B.C.E. Then later, when knights became a thing somewhere around the eight century, 700 - 799 AD, they lived by a code which included being virtuous.

The premise was that a person did not become a knight and then instantly had virtue. Having virtue made them knightly. Leadership follows the same pattern. A person does not become a leader based on a position in any hierarchy and then begins acting in leadership. A person acts in leadership, achieving the state of being a leader at that time.

We achieve the state or position of being a leader by acting in leadership. The BASIC Leadership platform defines when a person is acting in leadership. We have it reversed. A person does not become a leader based on a position in any hierarchy and then begins acting in leadership. A person acts in leadership, achieving the state of being a leader at that time. A person moves in and out of the state of being a leader their entire life.

A person does not become a leader based on a position in any hierarchy and then begin acting in leadership. A person acts in leadership, achieving the state of being a leader at that place in time. ~Scott M. Carter

WARNING!

A warning exists in chapter three and on the back cover of this book. You had a choice. You decided to continue. I warned you that once you read this book, you will never look at the concept of leadership the same way again. Gaining insight and changing your beliefs comes with challenges and a price one must pay. What is that price, you ask?

You are about to continue your journey of gaining a great deal of insight that illustrates that much of what we are being taught about leadership are myths, fads, and cliches. When you attend future leadership trainings or workshops, those venues have a very high probability of including leadership myths within the overall format. And many of the books you read or videos you watch are likely to contain similar myths.

The price you pay might be an aversion to reading any existing leadership books or attending leadership training. That is a steep price. We need to address that right now before we continue.

Please do not throw out the baby with the bath water. The baby bath water analogy teaches us that we want to look for the good things that have value and not toss everything into the trash without consideration for all the components. Therefore, when you read any book about leadership, watch any video, or attend any seminar or training, your focus will be to identify one or more valuable things that you can take away that will be helpful. There is still plenty of good to be found there. Keep the baby.

In the upcoming chapters, your viewpoint of what leadership is in its true essence will continue to be dramatically impacted. Do not let that dissuade you from seeking more knowledge. Do not get caught in that trap. Everything you think you know about the concept of leadership will be challenged. Now, let's move on to the next chapter, where we see an example of how some are finally getting it when it comes to leadership in its true essence.

CHAPTER THIRTEEN

Some are Finally Getting It

During my career, I've been to at least a dozen leadership training sessions arranged by the organizations where I was employed. It's 2018, and all the department heads, eleven in total, including myself, attended an offsite leadership training set up by Human Resources. The training resource used at this offsite is the book *The Leadership Challenge*, written by James Kouzes and Barry Z. Posner and first published in 1987.

Kouzes and Posner's platform is well established and has existed for thirty-five years when I began writing this book. Other successful authors highly praise the Leadership Challenge platform. These authors include Patrick Lencioni, who wrote *The Five Dysfunctions of a Team,* and Ken Blanchard, who has written a series of books based on *The One Minute Manager.*

In Kouzes and Posner's book, Chapter 13, titled *Leadership is Everyone's Business,* enlightens us on what they say about where leadership exists. If you've read this book, please tell us what they say. Most people probably never make it that far, completely ignore this chapter, or forget it because they have already moved on to another resource. At the point where I'm writing this paragraph, I grin because I realize that some people might be superstitious and not want to read a thirteenth chapter. I think somewhere in the massive, ridiculous list of hundreds of leadership definitions is the label of Superstitious Leadership. What do Kouzes and Posner say about leadership?

In their 1995 Edition of *The Leadership Challenge*, Kouzes and Posner define leadership as "the art of mobilizing others to want to struggle for shared aspirations." Sorry folks, but that's just business and sounds like the job responsibilities assigned to one or more positions in a hierarchy. If that were leadership, and we want more leaders, we'd all be running around frantically trying to mobilize others to struggle for our shared aspiration. Not much of anything would get done unless those following this advice are all in the same organization, driving toward an organizational objective. In other words, just doing business.

Their 1995 edition discusses leadership as not being attached to a position. However, by 2002 in the 3rd edition, they make a dramatic shift by clarifying where leadership exists. Kouzes and Posner say that leaders are people who live next store to us or sit in the cubicle next to us. They say leadership is not about a title or position. It's not about organizational power or authority. And most importantly, it's not about being at the top of any hierarchy, whether it's business, government, or military. The only place you must look is inward. Kouzes and Posner apply the label of "Everyday Leader" to these people and say they are just like you and me.

So, it's 2002, and Kouzes and Posner made a shift and more clearly defined where leadership truly exists. 2002 is also the beginning of the timeline when the internet changes how we can access information - an explosion of leadership materials that you and I will have to sort through to try and make sense of already complex subjects. Everything quickly gets lost in a sea of complexity. The complexity continues to rise at a staggering rate.

I began my research into the concept of leadership in 2016. I had come to the same conclusion as Kouzes and Posner before reading their book. Almost every resource I encountered up to that point still had leadership attached to the top positions in all hierarchies, and most resources continue to place it there. Those who state that it is not a position in any hierarchy then have trouble defining it. I ran into that same challenge. After completing my research and establishing that leadership was not a position in any hierarchy, the question of "what is leadership?" remained. If it is not a position or title, and if it is inward, and we all can possess it, then what is it?

While Kouzes and Posner tell us it is not a position in any hierarchy, the problem with ending it there is that any of the people telling us it is not a position in any hierarchy all have different attributes of what it means to be a leader or a different definition of leadership. Kouzes and Posner tell us we have to mobilize others to want to struggle for our shared aspiration. That's one of hundreds and hundreds of ways people are defining leadership.

Suppose that we're lucky enough to find multiple resources that tell us leadership is not a position in any hierarchy. Each resource gives us 3 or 5, or 7 different attributes or practices that define leadership. And here's the kicker, Kouzes and Posner's book and any other resource you find who agrees on leadership not being a position in a hierarchy are resources designed for people in business. And those reading them are at the top of the hierarchy. *The Leadership Challenge* is a business book about organizations. It says so in the title. The full title is *The Leadership Challenge: How to Make Extraordinary Things Happen in Organizations.* They say there is no guarantee that you won't get fired even if you do what they say, and that's because it's just business. Are you starting to see a pattern here?

Jim Collins, through his book, *How the Mighty Fall,* shows us how the best of the best crash and burn, even after they were built to last, and Kouzes and Posner tell us there's no guarantee either. I love Kouzes and Posner's work and their consistency in presenting the same five practices. Want your business to get better? Buy their book and utilize the concepts that fit your business. I highly recommend them.

The point is that we agree that leadership is not a position in any hierarchy. Take the work of Jim Collins, and combine it with Kouzes and Posner's works, and your business has a massive advantage for creating longevity over other organizations. However, making extraordinary things happen in your organization differs from what we're debating here. We're defining when a person is acting in leadership. Kouzes and Posner provide an example of platforms transitioning from leadership being a position in a hierarchy to just being. I applaud them, and you should praise them too.

Now, back to the leadership training I attended. When the eleven people who participated in this Leadership Challenge training in 2018 returned to work, those at the top called themselves the leadership team, defying what they presented in chapter thirteen of Kouzes and Posner's book.

I was part of that leadership team. I do not remember us ever getting that far or covering chapter thirteen in our training. I later learned that after that training, not one person used the book as a guide to continue practicing what we had learned. That's the problem. The premise that leadership is not a position in any hierarchy exists. It is in its infancy, going unnoticed, remains lost in the complexity surrounding the concept of leadership, or is being rebuked by those who currently wear the label of leader and reside at the top of hierarchies.

Even after removing the label of leadership from a position in any hierarchy, continuing to define leadership in a thousand different ways leaves leadership vulnerable to the fate of complexity, which determines its effectiveness. So now what?

I vividly remember the day I watched a video of Simon Sinek giving a talk about his book *Start with Why*, first published in 2009. In his book, he introduces the Golden Circle to his readers. During one of his presentations at a leadership conference, in a humble voice, Sinek tells the audience that the golden circle has been there all along, and all he did was codify it. The golden circle is a drawing consisting of three circles. The outer circle is labeled "What," the middle circle is labeled "How," and the inner circle is labeled "Why." The golden circle helps us to understand that most organizations know what they do, some know how they do it, and very few organizations know why they do what they do.

Sinek says that when you define your "why," the people in your organization will be more engaged, increasing your effectiveness. The golden circle is simplicity which leads to increased effectiveness. His golden circle applies to all of life, not just business. Sadly, business is the only place everyone tries to use the concept. It has fallen victim to being attached to business when it has much more potential.

I did what Sinek did. He codified getting to our why using the golden circle. I codified our ability to determine when a person is acting in leadership using the BASIC Leadership platform. After three years of studying resources dealing with the concept of leadership, I established the premise that leadership was misguidedly attached to the top position or positions of hierarchies and also misguidedly associated with doing business.

I illustrated how this happened as the theories about leadership were established and grew from the early 1900s to the 21st century. I did not create an acronym and then attempt to locate words that would fit the letters. It was more like I was in a scene from the movie *Harry Potter and the Chamber of Secrets*. In that movie, when Ron needed the sword of Gryffindor, it presented itself. The BASIC acronym presented itself to me after compiling the main components that consistently appeared within the stories related to leadership. A truly magical moment. Now all I need is a wand containing dragon's breath, then learn to flick and swish properly while I chant incantations. Where's Hermione when I need her.

The good news is that some are finally getting it. Leadership, in its true essence, has nothing to do with a position in any hierarchy or with doing business. Let's put a few misguided leadership myths to the test. We'll begin with one that doesn't require the BASIC Leadership platform to determine its illegitimacy.

CHAPTER FOURTEEN

Nobody is Following You

What do you think about the statement, "In order to be a leader, you must have followers?" Look behind you. Is anyone following you? If you asked the people who work where you work if they are followers, how do you think they would respond? How would *you* respond if someone asked you if you were a follower?

Why do you go to work? Answers to that question can differ, but they all fit into one category. In developed countries, we go to work because we live in monetary-based societies. Before money became the primary medium, we lived in bartering-based systems. Bartering is the exchange of goods or services for other goods or services without using money.

In the early 1600s, people used tobacco as currency. In 1642 the Virginia State legislature made tobacco a form of legal tender. People carried one-hundred-pound sacks of tobacco to the shipping docks to pay for the transport of others via ship. How different the opening scene in the movie *Titanic* would have looked if that was still the currency needed for that voyage?

We live in a monetary-based society, so I work to earn money to pay my mortgage, travel, and buy food and clothing. Sometimes how I use my money is a want, sometimes a need. In 2022 some societies still walk 1 to 3 miles a day to get water for their village. They go to work lugging water for survival. Who are they following? They are following a purpose, not a person. That's why they do what they do. Why do you go to work? Is it to follow someone, thereby making some other person a leader?

An organization, profession, or industry can have an admiral purpose attached to it. My wife, Lisa, works for a medical device company. The products they produce save lives. Working for that organization can provide a sense of purpose, whereas manufacturing potato chips— not so much.

Producers of potato chips are in business because people like me love potato chips. It's one of my simple pleasures. Healthy? Certainly not, but I will continue to eat them because I choose to do so. If you try to take my chips away, as they say in the movie *The God Father*, we'll go to the mattresses.

I am not acting in leadership when it comes to potato chips and my health. But, I am fully aware and choose not to act in leadership when I shovel down those crunchy delights. People who work for a potato chip manufacturer work there because it serves some purpose for them—mainly money which helps them to fulfill other more worthy ideals, such as feeding their families and paying their bills. Imagine what a real conversation might look like at a job interview if we told the truth.

"Why do you want to work here?" asks the interviewer. "I have children to feed, and you're hiring," responds the applicant, thinking, "what a dumb question. You make potato chips. Do you think producing potato chips is a noble cause, and one day a shrine will be erected in your honor?"

Of course, any sane person would answer with, "I heard XYZ Potato Chip company is a great place to work, and you have a terrific culture. That's the kind of place where I want to build my career." We answer that way because *it's just business.*

We use culture, pay, and benefits, among other criteria, such as location, to differentiate between two or more organizations and why we choose one company over another. Even if an organization or industry is fortunate enough to have a higher purpose, such as saving lives, people are not following the people at the top of the organization.

We may be passionate about a higher purpose, and we choose to work in some organization or industry that allows us to accomplish that higher purpose. But how did these companies, with or without a higher purpose, come to exist in the first place? And at what point does leadership come into the picture?

In chapter seven, we examined the story of Steve Jobs and Stephen Wozniak of Apple. I have a couple of questions for you. First, who were they following? Second, who was following them? HP wanted nothing to do with their design. They had no followers. Just the two of them on equal footing working together in a garage. They had no teams, no departments, no managers, no workers, and no factory. If we need to have followers to be leaders, then this means they were only leaders once they built the Apple organization and had people theoretically following them.

Jobs and Wozniak presented their idea to others, many of whom had no interest in pursuing it as a business venture. Businesses like IBM and other companies required people to wear suits to fit an image, to eat, sleep, and crap their company logo and mantra. Steve Jobs had long, unkempt hair and deliberately avoided the typical business garb of that era. He certainly wasn't a leader or leadership material if you asked any executive at IBM in the 1970s.

Why are people running around still saying that being a leader requires followers? The root word of lead is to travel. In the days when the term "lead" came to be, we know that they took their donkey with them when they traveled, so one can argue they had a follower. There's a business image you'll never get out of your head. It doesn't matter that, in this example, Wozniak and Jobs developed computers. We can ask the same questions about the start of any organization, industry, or worthy ideal.

It's December 17, 1903, and you're standing in a field in Kitty Hawk, North Carolina. You watch in awe as the Wright brothers succeed in manned flight. The flight went a distance of 852 feet, lasting 59 seconds. Who were the Wright brothers following? No organization, no hierarchy, no salary. Were the people helping the wright brothers following them, or were they following a worthy ideal?

What about Martin Luther King, Jr.? On August 28, 1963, more than a quarter million people participated in the historic march on Washington for freedom and equality. Did Dr. King have followers, or were the people following a cause, a worthy ideal, acting on that worthy ideal, and collaborating with others to achieve success? And were there times when they were unsuccessful, then gained insight, and that new insight impacted their beliefs? Is this worthy ideal still progressing? Yes, even today, globally, we continue the battle against racism.

What about the three people in the opening chapter of this book, Madoff, Jones, and Delvey? Everyone says Jones had followers. They called him a leader. 900 people died. I'll let you chew on that one for a bit. What about Madoff? People were interested in financial gain. Accumulating wealth is what they were following. They were all in the game of business to make money. Delvey's worthy ideal was achieving fame, which did not require acting in leadership.

Now we can add in the conflicting advice we get from people who instruct on the concept of leadership. In chapter three, I said that the misguided way we attached the concept of leadership to the top positions in a hierarchy, we ended up with a massive number of definitions, and we would also get conflicting and contradictory definitions and labels.

On the one hand, we say to be a leader, a person needs followers. At the same time, others who stand in front of audiences and talk about leadership also say that an organization must create a powerful why, a purpose that will continue to drive the organization into the future, and that purpose is what the people must follow.

We cannot say a person needs followers to become a leader, then turn our heads to the left and spew out something in direct contrast, such as needing to create a purpose that people will follow. People become confused about who or what to follow. Here's a question for you. When the CEO departs, is he or she suddenly never a leader, never acting in leadership because they no longer have these fictional followers?

In chapter eleven, you learned about the book, *The Peter Principle.* Do you know what subject Dr. Laurence Peter addresses in his book? The leader-follower myth. He says, "This is typical of the hierarchiological fallacies banded about in administrative circles." He is referring to the misguided belief that to be a good leader, you must be a good follower first. He disproves that myth. As Dr. Peter puts it, "how can the ability to lead depend on the ability to follow? You may as well say the ability to float depends on the ability to sink." His study of hierarchies shows that Nobody was following Anybody, but Somebody thought Everybody should be.

Everybody, Somebody, Anybody, and Nobody

> A long time ago, in the country of Mythos, four people, Everybody, Somebody, Anybody, and Nobody had a debate about whether followers were needed to get things done.
>
> Everybody thought Anybody could be following Somebody. Anybody had the capacity, and Nobody was unwilling to follow.
>
> Anybody could have been a follower. However, Everybody though it should be Somebody.
>
> Nobody told Anybody how it should work. Nobody followed through to ensure that Somebody would follow, while Everybody was busy trying to convince Anybody to be a follower.

Charles Osgood was a broadcaster on both radio and television for CBS news. Often referred to as the network's poet-in-residence, Osgood wrote The Responsibility Poem. Look up both the short and long versions, you will find his sarcasm about responsibility quite entertaining. He inspired me to create the follower poem.

When Everybody, Somebody, and Anybody are busy looking for their own followers, that leaves Nobody. I assure you that no matter what your title or status, Nobody is most certainly following you. It appears that followers are elusive as Big Foot and aliens from outer space. Some people seem to think they exist, yet no one has ever actually met one. Perhaps we'll find bigfoot, aliens, and followers living in utopia, and we can all move there.

CHAPTER FIFTEEN

Perfection & Utopia

Perfection does not exist. Everything has flaws. There is no such thing as a flawless diamond. It's marketing language. Look close enough under a very powerful microscope, and you'll find flaws. It's likely that there are errors in this book, the one you are reading right now. It has been edited multiple times by some very smart people, yet it will have flaws. I will leave those flaws once it is published. It serves as an example that illustrates several points being made throughout this book. I could edit it endlessly for perfection but then my next two books would never get written.

Humans, societies, and nature all have imperfections. Too often, we seek perfection where it does not exist or we cannot obtain it. Defining leadership is one of those areas. Some will attempt to use the BASIC Leadership platform to solve everything surrounding the concept of leadership. That will not happen. The worthy ideal is simplifying so we can more effectively define when a person is acting in leadership.

Chapter fourteen shows us how no one is following you. That is an excellent example of dispelling leadership myths. Influential leadership and inspirational leadership can be just as easily proven to be leadership myths. We will begin with those and move on to some that might stumps us a bit.

Influence is influence. A person in any position in a hierarchy or any societal status can influence people.

Inspiration is inspiration. Many things, including other people's actions can inspire us. Nature's beauty and magic can inspire people. Does that make nature a leader?

When a gang inspires a susceptible teenager to join, and to do bad things, is the person doing the influencing acting in leadership? I have yet to have a person answer "yes" to that question. And it is not a trick question. Yet, we have the labels of Gang Leader and Gang Leadership. Bernie Madoff influenced people through manipulation and the promise of big returns on their investments. What type of leadership was Jim Jones acting under when he influenced nine hundred people to commit suicide? Were Madoff and Jones acting in leadership? We can safely say, "No!"

Why can we come to that conclusion so quickly? It violates the integrity hub of the BASIC Leadership platform. Madoff had what he believed to be a worthy ideal: to get rich by deceiving others. He acted on it. Madoff gained insight on how to improve his deception and collaborated with others to continue the sham. How did he accomplish this? Influence and inspiration. Who *the bleep* knows what Jim Jones was thinking? He was just a whack-job. And we know Delvey wanted fame. She told us so herself. She inspired others through her fictitious foundation.

I read the book *Leadership and the Ethics of Influence* by Terry L. Price, published in 2020. Price works among the University of Richmond Ethics Working Group and the Jepson School of Leadership Studies faculty. Price wrote an entire book discussing the ethics of influence as it relates to leadership.

One part of the book contrasts Machiavellian ethics-based theory against Kantian ethics theory. Machiavellian refers to cunning, scheming, and unscrupulous. Kantianism refers to a philosophy of rational morality.

Price proposes arguments such as if a societal goal is moral, can a person manipulate others to achieve it? Have you ever heard the phrase, "The ends justify the means?" In simple terms, that phrase implies that we can override one level of morality to achieve what someone deems to be a greater moral goal. Things like this get debated for decades and never get solved. In the case of leadership, using the BASIC Leadership platform, we can easily define when we are acting in leadership for most things, but not everything.

When we apply things to the leadership lifeline, we can quickly identify when certain things fall on the positive or negative sides. On which side do responsibility and discipline fall? On which side do blame and neglect fall? We quickly knew the answers to those two questions.

On which side does risk fall? Risk can fall on both sides depending on how you view risk. The minute you are born, risk exists. Driving to work is risky. Having children is risky. Going into business is risky. Want to know how risky life is? You're not going to get out alive. Leadership is not about risk. Life is one big risk.

How about guilt? On which side of the Leadership Lifeline would you place guilt? Is guilt a negative thing because it implies wrongdoing? Sure it is. We say that a person is guilty of something. But why does guilt exist? It's built-in by nature as a way of telling us that we have done wrong. We *feel guilty*. It's an emotion supplied by nature. Guilt can prevent us from continuing to act in ways unbecoming a leader. We can therefore deduce that guilt is a positive thing. That is, until we see someone use guilt to influence others to do something-then, guilt becomes a negative thing. Now, where would you place guilt on the Leadership Lifeline?

How about shame? Where would you place that on the Leadership Lifeline? Again, nature provides us with some guidance. We *feel shame* for a reason. That reason is that we know we have done something unleaderly. We can also shame someone else into doing things. It can fall on both sides of the lifeline.

When testing against the BASIC Leadership platform, we will encounter concepts like risk, guilt, and shame that seem to elude us. But when we look more closely at them, we discover that "the application of each" defines where they fall on the leadership lifeline.

This will not be the case for everything. Like the character Neo in the movie *The Matrix*, you will get to make a choice. Take the red pill and learn a potentially unsettling, life-changing truth; not everything can be solved. Or take the blue pill and live in a dream world where we expect life to be perfect. What you believe will drive you to take action or not take action, moving you toward or away from a worthy ideal, gaining insight along the way, and collaborating to make things happen.

When we find a platform that will not solve everything, some discount any value it provides. We ask questions like, can the ruler of a country manipulate its people to achieve what is deemed a greater moral, societal goal? Sure, they can. But when doing so, it does not mean they are automatically acting in leadership. However, defining when a person is acting in leadership becomes easier when we remove leadership from a position in a hierarchy, and we do not seek Utopia.

The word Utopia comes from the Greek οὐ ("not") and τόπος ("place"). It means "not a place." Seeking perfection is the same as seeking Utopia. We continue to go down deep rabbit holes, crazy matrix-like dream worlds where many seek this mythical place. Now that we know the definition of Utopia, the reality is that when we seek perfection, we actually end up in Utopia.

We end up nowhere. When I attempted to perfectly define leadership, I entered that mythical world.

Sometimes life is like being trapped in an elevator. You're always going up or down, and all you want to do is get off. Most times you're not even the one pushing the buttons. Instead of defining leadership, we created a bunch of clichés.

CHAPTER SIXTEEN

Metaphors, Analogies, and Clichés

I will spill some of my inner sci-fi geek all over everyone again, as I did in my first book. I love *Star Trek*, *Star Wars*, and most other sci-fi series and movies.

In *Star Trek, The Next Generation* series, season five provides an episode called "Darmok." In this episode, Captain Picard ends up on a planet with another being that speaks English, but differently than we do on earth. In their culture, they talk in short sentences that might make no sense to humans here on earth.

For example, in this episode, a Tamarian named Dathon utters phrases such as, "Shaka, when the walls fell," then repeats it over and over without any other context. Imagine hearing that phrase, then another phrase, "Darmok and Jalad at Tanagra," again repeated without context, then "Temba, his arms wide," and

"Sokath, his eyes uncovered." That would seem strange to us. That is unless we discover we also do it.

We speak the same way and do not even realize it. Tamarians talk in metaphors, and so do we. "Shaka, when the walls fell" implies failure. "Temba, his arms wide" means giving or receiving. "Sokath, his eyes uncovered" indicates that a person understands. They see the point being made. It seems simple now that we know what those phrases mean. What does this have to do with our ability to understand leadership?

Much of what we experience in life is abstract. We use language to attempt to give concreteness to abstract things. Time is abstract. Sure, we can tell time. When we look at a clock, we know what time it is. However, time is constantly moving forward. Time is intangible, meaning it has no taste or smell, and we cannot feel, touch, or see time. To compensate for this abstractness, we give concreteness to time by talking about it like it is money.

Money is concrete. Money is a tangible item. We can see, feel, smell, and even taste it. However, I do not recommend putting paper or metal currency in your yapper. Using metaphors, we turn time from abstract and intangible to concrete and tangible. We *spend* our time doing things. You need to *budget* your time. These meetings *cost* me a lot of time.

Time is not ours to give to anyone. No one possesses time, yet we say we *give* our time, and we *trade* our time for money, We *make* time for things. No one can produce time like it is a product we manufacture.

We also use currency to help us relate to the concept of trust. We build a *trust account* with someone by exhibiting trustworthy behaviors. We must make *deposits* into that account. We say we *lost trust* in someone like a $20 bill fell out of our pocket. We use farming as an analogy to relate to how our lives work. We refer to our mind as a *farmer's field*. We *reap what we sow*. We must *plant* the right seeds in our minds for the right things to *grow*. We must remove the *weeds*, referring to negative thoughts, or those thoughts will keep our life *crops* from growing.

These metaphors and analogies work very well. Our mind doesn't care what we plant. Plant Nightshade, and it will grow. Nightshade contains poisonous alkaloids-one called solanine can be deadly. Thinking negative thoughts is like planting Nightshade. Instead, plant a crop you can harvest and use to serve a worthy ideal—plant positive thoughts and ideas.

"That's as useful as rearranging the deck chairs on the Titanic" is an analogy. That phrase implies that the suggestion offered will not save a sinking ship. It accomplishes nothing. "Life is like a box of chocolates. You never know what you're gonna get." One of the many famous lines from the movie *Forrest Gump*. It illustrates how life has many choices and surprises, and we can visualize how that happens with a box of mixed chocolates. Have you ever grabbed a piece of chocolate at random from an assorted box, take a bite, and then toss the other part of that chocolate out? "Life is a roller coaster of emotions" implies extreme highs and lows.

We can feel them by imagining being on a roller coaster. We use analogies as often as we use metaphors. Analogies also help us to relate to the abstract.

The time is money metaphor developed during the industrialization of the United States in the early 1900s. It then spread throughout the rest of the world, impacting how we view time, which is in terms of money. That has impacted our perception of time, thus driving the behaviors within our organizations. That is how powerful a metaphor can be in changing how we perceive the world and acting upon those perceptions.

Now, let's attempt to define leadership using a metaphor or an analogy. Just as time is money, leadership is _____. Could you fill in the blank with anything that makes the concept of leadership concrete? Does "leadership is influence" make the concept of leadership concrete? It does not. That's because the concept of influence is also abstract.

Influence is _____. Could you fill in the blank to help transition the abstract concept of influence into something concrete? How about leadership is inspiration? Does that metaphor help make leadership concrete?

We cannot see, smell, feel, or taste influence or inspiration. We took an abstract concept, leadership, and attempted to make it concrete using other abstract concepts. The idea behind metaphors and analogies is to take something abstract and allow us to understand it through an illustration using something tangible. The phrase "time is money" does that very well. Relating our minds to a farmer's field, planting thoughts does that very well. Just as metaphors like "time is money" appeared in the 1900s during the industrialization of the United States, the concept of leadership was on a similar journey where people were attempting to define it.

Look at the literature written about the leader-follower concept in terms of influence. The complexity is staggering. Then we add in the conflicting messages about where that influence exists, and we get an astounding level of confusion.

The leader, established by a position up the hierarchy, influences the follower, who resides lower down the hierarchy. Then suddenly, the follower influences the leader. This reversal is referred to as multidirectional influence. The influencing happens in both directions. Confusion sets in about who the leader is. Of course, we then get Multidirectional Leadership.

Let's take the hierarchy out of the equation—two people on equal footing. One person influences another, thereby making that person the leader. Now the other person influences the first person, and that person now becomes the leader. Can they both be leaders at the same time? If so, then where is the fictitious follower? Is the title of leader shifting back and forth? Is being a leader the same as acting in leadership? If leadership is influence, please help us understand this complexity and contradiction. Others have tried, and it's a deep, deep hole of complexity and confusion that one cannot dig out of no matter how hard one tries.

What about Fairness Leadership? Yep, there is a Leadership Fairness Model. Under the fairness approach to life, we started giving everyone a ribbon for participation. We give kids, and now adults, a trophy no matter how good or bad they are at something. The result of that? American kids have a delusional and unearned belief that they are smart or talented. They believe they deserve things without putting in time and effort to become good at anything. Then we wonder why we have issues at home, and when they enter the working world, we have problems in our organizations. Then we make up more crap in a misguided attempt to fix the problem we created. More leadership myths.

The newest made-up term that developed as I wrapped up writing this book? "Quiet quitting." It's the same as being disengaged. Instead of teaching leadership, which requires a person to take action toward a worthy ideal such as personal responsibility, putting in time and effort, gaining insight to become better at something, we teach our youth, and now adults, just the opposite under the label of Fairness Leadership.

We want fair wages, but no one can agree on what that means. We want work assignments distributed fairly across organizations when there is no way to accomplish that. We say life isn't fair, and that isn't true. It's a myth. The answer? Equal opportunity. Approaching life under the BASIC Leadership model provides equal opportunity. It is devoid of gender, race, ethnicity, or any other category we like to separate people into for other purposes. There is no such thing as Fairness Leadership.

Metaphors and analogies help us convert abstract concepts into tangible things we can relate to. A cliché is a phrase or opinion that is overused and betrays a lack of original thought. Leadership is influence has become a cliché. It does nothing to make the abstract concrete nor define leadership. Saying leadership is influence is as helpful as rearranging the deck chairs on the Titanic.

We did not know how to define leadership in concrete and tangible ways, so people developed intellectual soundings labels that solved nothing. We ended up with leadership is inspiration, leadership is influence, Fairness Leadership, and a cornucopia of other leadership types, which are myths. You can feel the label of Quiet Quitting Follower sneaking up on us. It's coming. These myths serve us no better than the misguided belief that to be a leader; one must have followers. Some myths do harm, while other myths teach us how to act in leadership.

Saying leadership is influence is as helpful as rearranging the deck chairs on the Titanic. ~Scott M. Carter

CHAPTER SEVENTEEN

Myths

A shepherd boy sat on a hillside watching over a flock of sheep. A boring task to some, so to entertain himself, the boy jumped up and yelled, "Wolf! Wolf! A wolf is chasing the sheep."

The villagers hurried up the hillside to help, only to find no wolf and a boy laughing at them because they came running when there was no wolf. The villagers warned the boy not to cry wolf when there is no wolf. This action will have consequences.

The boy did not listen to their warning. Soon he was bored again and yelled out that there was a wolf. When the villagers arrived up the hillside, they saw no wolf, just a grinning boy who had fooled them a second time.

Later that afternoon, the boy saw a real wolf approaching his flock. He sprang to his feet, yelling with all his might, "Wolf! Wolf! A wolf is chasing the sheep." This time the villagers did not respond to his call. They thought he was fooling them yet again.

When the boy did not return to the village with the sheep at sunset, they went up the hill to find him. He was weeping, the flock was scattered, and one of the sheep was missing. The boy wanted to know why they did not come when he called.

Aesop's Fables, or the Aesopica, is a collection of fables credited to Aesop, a slave and storyteller who lived in ancient Greece between 620 and 564 BCE. The boy who cried wolf is one of Aesop's fables. Fables are based on stories, often exaggerated to make a point. Fables are often referred to as myths.

We call the above story a fable or myth because perhaps this village boy and wolf scenario is based on a real-life experience, perhaps not. It's a mythical story that teaches the lesson that when you lie, especially often, this can lead to people not believing you even when you tell the truth. The characters' actions in mythical stories remind us how we should or should not behave.

Over the centuries, cultures around the world have developed mythical gods, heroes, and villains. The Norse god, Thor, has a mighty hammer and shoots lightning bolts from his eyes. The Greek god, Zeus, throws lightning bolts as if they were spears. When we look at different cultures from centuries ago, many had developed these mythical gods to explain weather and earthquakes. Fables and myths were used in many ways.

Oral storytelling is how societies and cultures pass down their history from generation to generation. What we overlook is how these fables and myths taught lessons in leadership. Communities preserved history for thousands of years through storytelling because most people in cultures worldwide could not fluently read or write.

Proof of the power of storytelling is all around us. The streaming platform Disney Plus offers a documentary series called *Drain The Oceans*. Scientists use sonar technology to map the ocean's bottom and create an incredibly realistic image in vast detail. Today's computer technology produces a powerful visual effect making it appear as though they actually drain the ocean.

In one *Drain the Oceans* episode, they look at the west coast of the United States, specifically the Washington State coast. Researchers determined, right down to the day, an underwater earthquake that destroyed the coastline in 1700. This seismic event sent a title wave to Japan's coast, where historians in Japan recorded it. It's the effort they went through to get to their findings that is relevant here.

Someone wondered if what they found in sediment layers on the Washington coast was evidence of a seismic event. They went all the way to Japan to check their records. At the end of this science and research, the narrator says they spoke with the local Indian tribes to see if they had any history of this occurrence. Sure enough, they did.

The local tribe responded by saying that the researchers could have just asked them. The local tribes have told the story of this event for generations. *It's not just a story*. They also teach a lesson through the story.

The lesson is to ensure you do not build your village close to the ocean.

Currently, over 10 million people live in an area on a coastline where it is highly likely that this event will happen again within the next 100 or so years. Too bad they weren't listening to the stories shared by those who know the power of stories. Of course, should that happen again, someone will scream, "climate change."

Leadership Myths

When we look up leadership myths in the twenty-first century, we get arguments about what works best in business. Participative versus authoritarian. It's an argument using McGregor's X and Y theory of leadership from his 1960 book, *The Human Side of Enterprise*. The title tells us it is about business because it says "enterprise." So whether we call it an article, a blog post, or any other format someone uses to disseminate these myths to us, it's an argument about what works best in business, not a debate about which approach constitutes leadership.

In their book *Leaders,* published in 1985, Warren Bennis and Burt Nanus outline the six myths of leadership. One of the myths listed in their book addresses the behaviors associated with McGregor's X and Y theories. The X theory portrays people as controlling and manipulating. Bennis and Nanus tell us that it's a myth that one is a leader by being controlling and manipulating. They say that leadership as an exercise in power is a myth.

Then we get to 2020, and when people put out an article on leadership myths, their list contains these same arguments, parroting what Bennis and Nanus said back in 1985. No originality, just clichés, and ones that pertain to business approach practices, not leadership in its true essence.

Leadership existing only at the top of an organization is also listed as one of Bennis and Nanus' six myths. If a person sees that language and has not read that entire segment addressing that specific myth, one might argue that others were saying that leadership was not a position in any hierarchy.

Notice the language used in my argument, which is "in any hierarchy." Bennis and Nanus said leadership doesn't exist at the very top of the organization, meaning only with the CEO. They illustrate how when an organization expands and creates more divisions, those at the top of those mini hierarchies within the main hierarchy can also be leaders.

In short, a person still needs to be at the top of some form of hierarchy, even a small one, to be a leader. Based on that argument, to have more leaders, an organization must grow and create more mini hierarchies to produce more leaders. They were still attaching leadership to the top of a hierarchy and may have yet to realize it. Most arguments labeled as leadership myths address myths about what is most effective for accomplishing organizational objectives. That's just business.

It's 1991. Joseph C. Rost published his book *Leadership for the Twenty-First century*. Rost studies hundreds of resources consisting of books, journal articles, and white papers (studies) from 1900 to 1979. The premise of his research?

> To determine if, by the end of the 1970s, the study of leadership helped us better understand the concept of leadership and to define it.

Rost argues that any assumption about making advancements in defining leadership is a myth. See the difference between arguing a leadership myth and a business myth? Rost presents a leadership myth. He says that any statements people make regarding progress being made in defining leadership up until 1979 is a myth.

We ended up with leadership is influence. Leadership is inspiration. Leadership requires followership. Leadership is _____. Fill in the blank. There are hundreds and hundreds of definitions, including types and styles of leadership. Here's the real kicker. Rost's research uncovered that most of the books, journals, and white paper studies for 80 years did not define leadership. Want to know why? That's because a person cannot define leadership, and no one ever will. We can only define when a person acts in leadership.

> *We cannot define leadership, and no one ever will. We can only define when a person acts in leadership.*
> ~Scott M. Carter

Rost also attempted to go on to define leadership, and he failed because it is not possible. I tried, and I failed. Here is where Rost and I agree wholeheartedly. When the concept of leadership is anything anyone wants to say it is, the concept of leadership is meaningless. And we weren't the first to say that. Chester Barnard published his first book in 1939, *The Functions of the Executive.* He understood leadership to be separate from business. In 1948 Chester Barnard said, "Leadership has been the subject of an extraordinary amount of dogmatically stated nonsense." Dogma refers to a principle or set of principles laid down by an authority as incontrovertibly true. What do you, the reader, think about that statement? Would you be bold enough to make that statement? Or are you bold enough to take the BASIC™ Leadership challenge and define leadership?

No other topic in the behavioral sciences has been more studied and written about than leadership. In chapter three we learned of Ralph M. Stogdill. He produced the *Handbook of Leadership: A Survey of Theory and Research,* the granddaddy of leadership books. This book's first of four versions contains 429 pages, with 150 pages providing over 2,800 resource references. By the third edition in 1990, this book is a massive 914 pages of copy, with 190 additional pages containing over 7,500 resource references. The 1980s saw an incredible increase in the number of books addressing leadership. Some estimates say over 100.

In my opinion, we see leadership clichés splattered all over the place based on myths. Leadership is influence. Leadership is inspiration. Leadership is _____. Fill in the cliché. These are myths. One cannot define leadership and never will. We can define "acting in leadership" and have been for centuries through stories passed down from generation to generation. "The Boy Who Cried Wolf" is an example. Does acting in leadership exist within the BASIC Leadership platform, or are some people just lucky?

CHAPTER EIGHTEEN

Lucky or BASIC?

Lucius Annaeus Seneca was a Roman philosopher born over two thousand years ago in 1 BCE. Seneca was Spanish, educated in philosophy, and had a dramatic political career in Rome. Do you know what Seneca said thousands of years ago? "Luck is what happens when preparation meets opportunity."

Luck is what happens when preparation meets opportunity. ~Lucius Seneca

You even need to be prepared to win the lottery. That's right. If you never buy a ticket, you cannot win. Bad odds? Absolutely. Extremely lucky if you hit those odds? Absolutely. Most financial experts will advise that it is a waste of money. But if you never buy a ticket, can you win? Absolutely not.

So how does life work? How do you buy a lottery ticket to life? How can you increase your odds of winning in life? If we define success as hitting the immense jackpots of being famous and having lots of money, then the odds are very similar to the lottery. If that is your goal, then like buying a lottery ticket, you need to put yourself in a position to win.

That's an intriguing perspective on how things work, don't you agree? Looking for a winning lottery ticket in a game that isn't a lottery, is like going on a wild goose chase. Life isn't a lottery, and fortunately, we are not defining success in terms of the accumulation of wealth and material things. However, ask anyone who has achieved anything in life how they did it. What do you suppose they might say?

Colin Powell said, "There are no secrets to success. It is the result of preparation, hard work, and learning from failure." Colin Luther Powell was an American politician, statesman, diplomat, and United States Army officer who served as the 65th United States Secretary of State from 2001 to 2005. He was the first African American Secretary of State. He tells us how he achieved his success. The BASIC Leadership platform is how you put yourself in a position to win at life, no matter what you list as your worthy ideal. You can't win if you don't play.

Other people are not lucky. That's an excuse we use not to take action. It comes from a mindset, a belief of how others achieved things. When people talk about luck, they use words like chance. People who progress toward an ideal and reach levels that others do not, those people talk about opportunity.

When a person thinks of themselves as unlucky, that mindset will work against the power of the BASIC Leadership platform. Lucky people create, notice, and act upon the potential opportunities in their lives. They don't believe in luck. They know that their beliefs drive the actions they take. Those actions lead to outcomes. Sometimes the results end in forward progress, and sometimes they do not. In either case, it provides insight into what to do more of, what not to do again, or how to do something better or differently. When a person does the same thing repeatedly, expecting different results, then the insight component has been missed. That's the definition of insanity—*Doing the same thing over and over again and expecting different results.*

You will only be lucky if you set a path toward the worthy ideals of getting healthy, physically, mentally, financially, or in any aspect of your life. That's because, as Seneca said, luck is what happens when preparation meets opportunity. BASIC is the formula for life. It is a progression that requires a person to be intentional. After all, we have the label of Intentional Leadership.

Yep, there is a Center for Intentional Leadership, invented and started by someone. I have a news flash for you. The only way you progress toward any goal, any worthy ideal, is to be intentional about it. You're always headed somewhere in life. Life moves forward. There is no stopping it. It's going to happen to everyone who is born. No matter what happens in your life, do you know the one common factor always present? The only common factor in every part of your life is *you*. Do you know how this book, the one you are reading right now, came to be?

When I began this journey in 2016, my goal was to write a business book. I believed I could create something that would solve all the issues that continued to plague the workplace. I had looked at most other platforms, saw what I deemed to be flaws, and decided to look at ways to fix them. What happened from the time I started that journey, up to producing the book you are reading now, follows the BASIC Leadership platform.

I believed in something, a worthy ideal. I acted on those beliefs. I progressed over time, moving forward in some instances and making no progress at other times, including going backward a bit. I gained insight and collaborated with others. Throughout the entire journey, I moved randomly from one component to another within the BASIC Leadership platform.

After six months, I was close to having a book manuscript ready to go. Then I hit a roadblock. When I reached the point of talking about leadership, the subject became complex. Unlimited definitions and hundreds and hundreds of labels, many of which conflicted with one another, left me at a standstill. That changed the path of my journey.

One of the many things I had read about in books had now become a reality in my life. When we want to reach a destination or a goal, we often lay out the path we think will get us there. Then as we begin that journey, our path changes. It's like your GPS saying, "recalculating." The scenery starts to look different than we envisioned, and the characters change, like actors leaving and entering the stage during a play. That recalculation requires us to move within the BASIC components like a Wonkavator.

I acted, gained insight into the complexity associated with the concept of leadership, and now, new insight would change my path. The next three years of my life would be spent researching the concept of leadership. Rather than producing a business book, several other things would happen.

First, I would create The Loop of Optimal Effectiveness, which illustrates how a rise in complexity impacts effectiveness. I wasn't lucky in developing that concept. I was prepared when the opportunity presented itself. See the difference? Second, I would write and publish a research book, *Leadership: Achieving Optimal Effectiveness*, and then third, write and publish this book, the one you are reading right now. Not only did those things transpire, but an entire series of additional books also are in the works. *The Bible Teaches Acting In Leadership*, a satirical book about leadership myths, which has yet to be named, and several others I will not reveal here.

Those books will exist because, through my actions and the insight gained, opportunities presented themselves. None of those things, the Loop of Optimal Effectiveness, the research book, this book, and the future books, were on my "to-do" list. These opportunities appeared because of how the BASIC Leadership platform naturally operates. Luck is what happens when preparation meets opportunity. When we act in leadership, we are always in the state of preparation.

> *Luck is what happens when preparation meets opportunity. When we act in leadership, we are always in the state of preparation.* ~Scott M. Carter

I am no smarter than anyone reading this book. I possess no special skills that you, the reader, or anyone else, do not possess. I was not raised in a wealthy family. I worked full-time while doing the research and writing and producing these books. I do not have more time than you. We all have twenty-four hours in a day.

The difference between people's lives is that anyone you've heard of who did anything that improved their lives, including myself, operated under the BASIC Leadership platform to progress toward a worthy ideal. Some did not act in leadership, and we know who they are by the stories told about them. The BASIC outer ring alone is how life works, how a progression toward a worthy ideal happens. Acting in leadership requires passing through the integrity hub and operating on the positive side of the leadership lifeline. The good news is that the BASIC Leadership platform *works for everyone.*

I also have some bad news for you. Your life is going forward whether you want it to or not. Life does not stop happening. If you do not live your life under the BASIC Leadership platform, then life *will* happen *to you.* There were periods in my life when I let life happen *to me.* Then when I learned that I had control over that, things changed. If you are not making plans for your life, someone else is. Do you know what they have planned for you? *Not much.*

> *If you don't design your own life plan, chances are you'll fall into someone else's plan. And guess what they have planned for you? Not much.* ~Jim Rohn

My story of how this book came into existence mirrors the path of many of the business stories we read. PayPal was established initially as Confinity in 1998 by Max Levchin, Peter Thiel, and Luke Nosek. They began by developing security software for handheld devices. Security software for handheld devices was their initial plan, their objective, and their worthy ideal. That did not pan out. Instead, they changed directions leading them into the digital wallet software industry. In March of 2000, Confinity merged with x.com, an online financial services company founded by Elon Musk, Harris Fricker, Christopher Payne, and Ed Ho.

That was not the same path that Levchin, Thiel, and Nosek started on. They changed direction. The second thing would not have occurred without the first thing. Life and business plans may change or shift, but the process under which it happens is always the same. Their beliefs were challenged, and their worthy ideal shifted, but the BASIC process never stopped. Belief, action, success, insight, and collaboration. They moved in and out of the BASIC components of the outer wheel like they were in a Wonkavator.

Is there anything in your life that has not followed this pattern? Let's take it right down to the basics of life. When we are toddlers attempting to walk, we believe we can because we see others doing it. Walking is a worthy ideal. We then act on it. We try over and over, constantly falling, then eventually we progress toward walking more consistently. Throughout life, we still fall occasionally; especially if you live in Minnesota, where I reside. Snow and ice can make our routine walking skills quite challenging. We even fall upwards when climbing steps as adults. We never reach 100% perfect walking capacity. We never stop progressing toward walking effectively. We do it on autopilot, subconsciously, because it has become a habit. No one ever gives up on learning to walk, yet for some reason we stop progressing toward worthy ideals in other areas.

Did someone give you your ability to walk upright? We followed the BASIC outer wheel; otherwise, we'd all still be crawling around. Likewise, do you think someone has to give you leadership? Or is it yours for the taking?

The Film sensation *The Wizard of Oz* played in theaters for the first time in 1939, then aired on TV for the first time in 1956. The song lyrics "Follow the yellow brick road," is probably playing in your head right now.

The main character, Dorothy, played by Judy Garland, thought that her happiness could be found *out there somewhere.* You don't go looking for happiness, it's already yours. During her adventure to seek this happiness, she encountered a Scarecrow, a Lion, and a Tinman.

Each of those three characters also sought something. No, the Scarecrow was not looking for his gender identity, hoping the Tinman would notice him. The Scarecrow was looking for a brain, the Lion some courage, and the Tinman a heart. They learned of a wizard who might be able to help them. The wizard didn't give the Scarecrow, the Lion, or the Tinman anything they didn't already have. All three already had a brain, courage, and a heart. No one had to give those things to them.

When we believe we are intelligent and capable of learning, and we believe that courage already exists within us, and we have hearts that tell us we can achieve great things, then we can achieve great things. When our actions pass the integrity test and fall on the positive side of the leadership lifeline, we act in leadership. No one gives you leadership. You'll quickly discover that no one who achieved anything was lucky. We hear myths about the right place and time; there were more opportunities then, and how those opportunities are all gone now. All bovine scat, B.S. —Excuses to not make any effort at all.

The good news? You and I won't have to deal with flying monkeys. The bad news? Others are still trying to convince us that they allow us to be leaders, but we must first be followers. Someone will influence and inspire us so we can learn how to influence and inspire others, teaching us how to become leaders.

Yeah, that's it. Let's all go fight off winged chimpanzees while seeking that mythical wizard behind the curtain who can give us all leadership. No one can give you leadership except you. You can be a leader at any time in your life, which is done by acting in leadership.

The truth is incontrovertible. Malice may attack it, and ignorance may deride it, but in the end, there it is. — Winston Churchill

CHAPTER NINETEEN

Different or the Same?

Have you been to a leadership training or read any leadership books? What do the speakers or writers talk about regarding leadership? Yes, one can easily find hundreds of videos on YouTube, each one addressing a different topic. A random list of topics might include how leadership is about believing in yourself, respect, acting ethically, leaders have integrity, a desire to learn, they take action, and leaders have courage.

Now, look at videos or books that we categorize as personal development. We find the authors and presenters discussing the same subjects and concepts. We must believe in ourselves, be honest, act respectfully, act ethically, live life with integrity, and have the desire to learn. Successful people take action and have courage.

We teach the same things under two labels, leadership, and personal development. Let's look at two scenarios. Would you label the first as leadership or as personal development? And how would you label the second scenario?

Scenario one

My wife Lisa had her children attend Financial Peace University, where Dave Ramsey teaches common sense about money, including designing a financial plan. Ramsey teaches people about creating a budget at home. It's not complicated, and it is not new. The lessons are simple. Do not spend more than you make, don't accumulate debt, save for emergencies, and ultimately make wise decisions with your money. Taking action, being responsible, and grow through learning, aka gaining insight. When a person does these things, would you label this as personal development, or acting in leadership?

Scenario two:

The objective of a credit card company is to get people to carry debt. Credit card companies are "for profit" entities. Organizations that provide products or services to consumers must make a profit to continue to exists. Credit card companies profit from the interest they charge for their services. They use marketing to drive behaviors beneficial to their organization. Nothing unusual or complicated about either of those things.

Remember, the objective of a credit card company is to entice people to carry debt. If no one carried debt and paid interest to these organizations, they would cease to exist. What credit card companies offer to consumers appears counterintuitive to being financially responsible and acting in leadership. Assuming we agreed that the person in scenario one is acting in leadership.

I spent a decade in the finance world reviewing applications for financing. The people who paid cash for things, did not have credit cards, and had no debt payment history were deemed *not creditworthy* (I know how you feel. A great novelist couldn't make this crazy stuff up). These people could show they had money in the bank and assets such as a home paid in full. Yet, others who were leveraged to the hilt but made timely payments qualified for better programs and rates. *Wait a second here!* The people without credit scores were the most responsible with their money and finances, and they were being punished for that? Yep, because they never went into debt, they had no credit score.

Credit card companies operate under similar guidelines as home financing companies. They use credit scores to determine what rates they offer to a potential borrower. Being responsible with your money equates to being viewed as riskier? This defies common logic.

Are the people associated with operating a credit card company acting in leadership? Or is it just business?

Leadership, Personal Development, and Doing Business

We teach the concepts of taking responsibility for our actions, acting with integrity, taking action, having courage, and many other behaviors under both leadership and personal development. Yet, when we are "doing business" under the guise of leadership, many of the objectives set by organizations are in direct contrast to what we teach people to do under the label of personal development and the label of leadership. This simply does not make sense.

I've used Jim Rohn quotes several times in previous chapters. If you're not familiar with Jim Rohn, Rohn was the recipient of the 1985 National Speakers Association CPAE Award for excellence in speaking. His journey to receive that award began in the 1960s, leading Rohn to become one of, if not the premier business philosophers of all time. Many writers use the label of personal development when referring to Rohn. What does he call himself? A success counselor. Look up his distinguished career as a speaker, and you'll find the names of organizations you'll quickly recognize.

For over forty years, Rohn had been telling organizations, "There are no new fundamentals. You've got to be a little suspicious of someone who says, 'I've got a new fundamental.' That's like touring a factory where they manufacture antiques."

Instead of the basics, the fundamentals, people attempted to convince people that there were some *new* fundamentals that would solve all their woes. The separation between leadership and personal development occurs because we try to define leadership in terms of business, and we attach leadership to a position in a hierarchy. People were attempting to create new business fundamentals and labeling them as forms of leadership. We end up back at the title of chapter ten; *It's Just Business.*

Remember, from chapter one, your objective was to define leadership under two options.

Option 1: you get to draw from everything that exists about the concept of leadership and use it to define leadership.

Option 2: You get to start from scratch. Under the premise that everything we know about leadership, everything you've read, heard, or watched about leadership up to this point does not exist.

How would you define acting in leadership? Do you include what experts talk about under the label of personal development? Would you be able to distinguish between which concepts fall under leadership and which fall under personal development? Wait to answer. Read on first.

CHAPTER TWENTY

Fads, Fads, Fads

Do you know what the definition of a fad is? Fad; an intense and widely shared enthusiasm for something, especially one that is short-lived and without basis in the object's qualities; a craze.

The last part hits home, *short-lived and without basis in the object's qualities.* There are almost as many fads regarding getting physically healthy as there are made-up definitions of leadership. Everything from what we eat to how we get exercise, or in some cases, how to get fit without any physical activity at all. Here are some that gained popularity through the decades of the 1900s.

- 1920s The Cigarette Diet
- 1930s The Grapefruit Diet
- 1940s The Master Cleanser Diet
- 1950s The Cabbage Soup Diet

- 1960s The Drinking Man's Diet
- 1970s The Sleeping Beauty Diet
- 1980s The Scarsdale Diet
- 1990s The Atkins Diet

Crazy right? You could inhale smoke constantly into your lungs to achieve that thin model body. You could drink your way to becoming Charles Atlas and slumber your way to having a fitness model body. No wonder Sleeping Beauty looks so great in all her animated films. Elimination, juicing, meat-only, and rabbit food plans are still prevalent in the second decade of the 21st century.

I would love to say that we have learned a lot over the last 100 years regarding maintaining a healthy body, but that would be a lie. It seems that, in many instances, history just keeps repeating itself. We fall prey to fad after fad when it comes to our health and have fallen into the same trap with leadership. I wonder if the label Slow Learner Leadership exists.

Getting and staying healthy takes time and effort. It's easy. Saying things are "hard" is a mindset—a mindset derived from beliefs. Then we act on those beliefs by doing nothing or doing too much of the wrong things. At the end of your life, you will wish for more time. The time you could spend with loved ones, volunteering somewhere, or simply enjoying a sunrise or sunset. You cut your life short because you didn't act in leadership.

It is possible that a man could live twice as long if he didn't spend the first half of his life acquiring habits that shorten the other half. ~Socrates

Getting and staying healthy is a worthy ideal that requires the right mindset, taking action to accomplish it, gaining insight on how to do it effectively, collaborating with others to make it a reality, and doing so with integrity (no steroids, drugs, or short cuts), which gives you peace of mind. It's a lifelong progression toward a worthy ideal. A progression toward staying healthy never stops. It's not a magical, "ok, I arrived, I can stop eating healthy and become inactive."

If goal setting is part of leadership, those goals are supposed to move us toward something positive, and you do not have health goals, then are you acting in leadership?

We need to ask the same questions regarding our mental health. Physical health is only one-half of the equation. When we address mental health here, we are referring to the pursuit of changing the way we perceive things and continuing to educate ourselves. That's why we often use quotes from personal development and leadership coaches such as Dr. Wayne Dyer and Brian Tracy.

When you change the way you look at things, the things you look at change. ~Dr. Wayne Dyer

You cannot control all of what happens to you, but you can control your attitude toward all of what happens to you. ~Brian Tracy

Choosing to be happy and grateful rather than disappointed and bitter are examples of what Dyer and Tracy refer to when they address our beliefs.

If you need therapy, seek help. We should take mental health seriously. However, for most of society, we create the stress that exists in our lives. We can deal with stress by learning not to create it. You know what question is coming next, right? Do you have any written goals to achieve the worthy ideal of improving your outlook on life and decreasing stress levels?

Grab a giant stack of leadership and personal development books, and you'll see that they both talk about the same things regarding what leaders do. Leaders seek out knowledge and have the willingness to learn. Leadership is about a shift in paradigms. Paradigm is a fancy word for "our basic assumptions and the way we think." Stephen Covey, who wrote the book *The 7 Habits of Highly Effective People*, addresses the subject of paradigms in many of his live presentations.

Covey published his book in 1989, with a twenty-fifth anniversary edition in 2004. Who wrote the foreword to that anniversary edition? Jim Collins. Collins writes the foreword for what is labeled a personal development book and tells us that Bill Gates and Warren Buffet, among others, follow these steps. Covey's 7 habits book is considered a personal development book, with a forward written by an author who studies businesses. These are the kinds of things that began to stand out during my research.

It will be difficult for you to read these books or watch videos and not see the odd contradictions about any separation between leadership and personal development. You will begin to shift your beliefs.

Leaders shift their assumptions and the way they think. How do they do this? By gaining insight. How do they gain insight? By taking some action toward accomplishing that goal. Why do they take that specific action? Because gaining insight is a worthy ideal within itself. Will they likely collaborate with others to gain this insight to make a shift? Yes. Does this worthy ideal fall on the positive side of the leadership lifeline? Yes. Can anyone do these things? Yes. See how easy this is?

Fads and Health

Using 2017 – 2018 data, the National Institute of Diabetes, NIH, and Digestive and Kidney Diseases says that more than 2 in 5 adults (42.4%) have obesity, and about 1 in 11 adults (9.2%) have severe obesity. Wow! We live in the most technologically advanced country in the world, with access to healthy foods and ways to get exercise, and yet this is the state of our society when it comes to being healthy. *Yikes!*

What does the NIH list as the primary factors? Type and amounts of foods and drinks consumed; level of physical activity; and sleep habits. Yes, genetics can play a role, but a minor one. They also include access to and the ability to afford healthy foods. I say hogwash on those last two things unless you live in a third-world country. While overall health may be at a lower level in third-world countries, how many overweight people do you see in those places? How may obese ninety year olds do you see?

Getting physically healthy is easy. You eat reasonable portions, eat healthy foods, and exercise. How do you know when you are acting in leadership when it comes to being healthy physically? You know the answer. Are you doing the things it takes? And to be clear here, we are not talking about looking like the models that ad agencies splash all over the place that can make people feel self-conscious.

There are many body types, tall, short, thick, thin, slow metabolism, fast metabolism, and on and on. Don't give me that "it's genetics" crap. It doesn't matter which type you are. Acting in leadership is about you moving in a healthy direction, progressing toward a healthier *you*, not looking like a model in an ad or comparing yourself to others. Now, I'll ask the same question. Are you doing what it takes to become a healthier version of yourself?

Are you acting in leadership if you sit down and overeat on any type of food? You know the answer. When you head to the grocery store's checkout and look down at your cart, what do you see? Are you acting in leadership when you load your cart with sodas, cookies, microwave dinners, ice cream, and other tasty treats that you know will make you gain weight? And if you can afford those things, then access and affordability to healthy foods is not the issue.

The products we buy these days mislead us. Most items have some "low fat" or other fat-related languages on the label with some sort of vendetta and war on fats. Then they load the products with sugars in various forms. There are around 56 different names for sugars we put into our foods, including dextrose, fructose, galactose, glucose, maltose, and sucrose, or any variation of those names. I failed to find a local store selling beef jerky that was not loaded with sugar. Look at the labels on the condiments we put on our foods. Stop eating all that crap, and get educated on how to eat healthier, which does not require a person to turn into a rabbit chewing on lettuce and carrots. This book is not a health book. It's a leadership book. Start acting in leadership. That requires taking action, gaining insight, collaborating with others, and moving toward *the worthy ideal of a healthier you.* Be wary of fads.

Follow the Money

Diet and weight loss have grown to be a $71 billion industry. Yet, according to studies, over 95% of diets fail. We see a similar pattern with leadership and its fads. According to Absolute Reports, the global leadership training market reached $37.6 billion in 2021. Absolute Reports breaks leadership training out by country and the dominant players in the market.

What would you expect to find when you see the names of the leadership training platforms on their list? We find names that align with many of the authors of what we refer to as personal development books, including Carnegie, Covey, and Blanchard. We transition from entirely separate leadership and personal development categories to completely melding the two into leadership training platforms. During the development of leadership theories and attempts to understand leadership, leadership ended up being associated with business and attached to a hierarchy. For a period, they were different but the same. And now, based on the well-known leadership training platforms, they are the same.

Am I saying that all of these leadership platforms are fads? Not exactly. Many foundational principles regarding behaviors taught or coached are incredibly beneficial. Remember, don't throw the baby out with the bath water. But, and it's a big *but*, if these are not fads, why do most organizations bounce from one platform to the next? It's the same reasons that people bounce from one health fad to the next. Why is obesity such a big problem? Why are so many people in debt? Why is there a rise in suicides and antisocial behaviors? And why isn't the world filled with leaders acting in leadership?

Billion dollar industries are built on fads. Remember our definition of a fad. An intense and widely shared enthusiasm for something, especially one that is short-lived and without basis in the object's qualities; a craze.

There is a craze right now. A widely shared enthusiasm for something. In this case, it's an enthusiasm for overusing clichés and myths and how one can become a leader.

How did you react?

When I walk into the facility where my wife and I work out, there is a large sign on the wall as you come down the stairs from the second floor. That sign tells us to get healthy in body and mind. That's because those two things go hand in hand. Our beliefs play a crucial role in being physically healthy. I intentionally put the mindset part after the physical aspect of the discussion.

What was your reaction when you read what I said above about what you eat, exercise, genetics, access to healthy foods, affordability, and sleep habits? Did you immediately come up with excuses? Is it your genetics, lack of time, or other reason? Does your ethnicity, gender, or other any other personal trait prevent you from acting in leadership? The answer is "no."

Based on the answer to that question alone, any race or gender-based leadership label should not exist. Acting in leadership is the same for all of us. Did you justify your situation or someone else's? If so, you violated what the experts tell us are the mindset traits of leadership.

What are we told about leadership? Leaders do not make excuses. Leaders look for solutions. Leaders lead by example. Leaders never give up. Leaders are open-minded and creative. Leaders are flexible. Leaders are steadfast. Leadership is about responsibility and dependability. Leadership is about strategic and critical thinking. Leadership is about self-awareness. Leadership is about prioritizing. Leadership is about patience.

Leadership is about making decisions. Leadership is about continuous improvement.

Did we end up creating fads because we did not and still do not understand the basics of what constitutes acting in leadership? And that's because we have been attempting to define leadership when that is impossible to accomplish.

We thought we could smoke our way to a thin body and sleep our way to beauty. Now we can become leaders by acquiring followers, influencing, or inspiring people. I have a leadership coaching platform that teaches us how to create followers. Want to buy it? No? But wait, there's more! I'll throw in a free copy of drinking your way to thinness.

Like health, I would love to say that we have made progress over the last 100 years regarding leadership, but that would be a lie. It seems that, in many instances, history just keeps repeating itself. We fall prey to fad after fad when it comes to our health and have fallen into the same trap with leadership.

We separated personal development and leadership, and we created fads. Lots and lots of fads. Organizations bounce from one thing to the next, from fad to fad, with little or no impact. People hop from one fad to the next with little or no long-term results. Fads that have now become clichés. How many leadership clichés did you hear others vomit up in the last month? I'm surprised someone hasn't come out with a leadership drug or enchanted potion so we can avoid what acting in leadership requires of a person. After all, that's what we do with health. Take this drug and wrap that gismo around your waist to magically get slimmer.

We must be practicing Shortcut Leadership through those behaviors. Think I just made that up? Nope. There's an abundance of platforms, many of which interact with some of the most prominent organizations, and those leadership coaching companies have course segments labeled Leadership Shortcuts. I have one printed out. I put it with my copy of the cigarette diet.

In chapter nineteen we addressed finances and leadership, and in this chapter we addressed health and leadership. Are you up for the challenge of talking about what leadership means in terms of relationships? Should we even go there at this point? How messy might that get? But let's do it anyways so we can engage in Sadistic Leadership.

CHAPTER TWENTY-ONE

Transformers Participate in Authoritarian Collaborative Transactional Servantship

Relationship Leadership. Does it exist? It does according to leadership theories and many current-day leadership coaching platforms. Is there anything about life that doesn't require some kind of relationship? Once we headed down the path of Relationship Leadership, we dug deeper and deeper and deeper into a well of complexity.

Have you taken a personality profile test where you work? *Psychology Today* reports that about 80% of Fortune 500 companies use personality tests to vet for upper-level positions. When you read that, what comes to mind? Did you think they were testing to see if people were of sound mind? Not even close.

By the time we hit the 1940s, Katharine Cook Briggs and her daughter Isabel Briggs Myers created and published their personality profile questionnaire, known as the Myers-Briggs personality types. Potential candidates answer a series of questions. Our answers separate us into sixteen different personality types. The Myers-Briggs platform sprang from the works of Carl G. Jung in the 1920s. Jung developed the four personality types we see in the DiSC personality profile testing, Dominance—Influence—Steadiness--Conscientiousness.

Any idea how many definitions of leadership might develop from 16 personality types, and how they impact relationships? To start, each of the four DiSC labels is a type of leadership. Look them up. We already covered leadership is influence. If that's true, is leadership also dominance, steadiness, and conscientiousness?

Do any of these four or sixteen personality profile labels increase or decrease a person's ability to act in leadership? The answer is "no." Instead, we argue over which personality profile is best for... ready for it... drum roll please... here it comes... *for our business.*

Should we put a person into a managerial or executive role who is more likely to use an authoritarian or participative approach? Or perhaps we should use a transactional approach? We continue talking about approaches to business, not leadership in its true essence. We have it backward. Changing or impacting relationships does not make a person a leader. Acting in leadership affects our relationships.

We continue talking about approaches to business and not about leadership in its true essence. ~Scott M. Carter

Know what happens when you set financial goals and progress toward being financially responsible? Your current and future relationships will be impacted. How will they be affected? You will no longer want to be around others who are not financially responsible.

When people constantly call you to go out on the town, to go shopping because they love to shop, to spend money randomly, you will do less of those things or stop doing them altogether. Because you are no longer their shopping or party buddy, they will begin to call you less often and find someone else who will go with them.

This transformation will happen organically because you now have financial goals. We are not talking about getting rich or wealthy, nor about having to stop doing fun or social things. It's about how acting in leadership will impact relationships.

Begin to change your eating habits, and that change in practices will impact your current relationships. You start bringing a healthy lunch to work, and those who eat out daily, the ones who ask what fast food you want today, will ask you less often. When ordering out and eating unhealthy foods is one of the central premises of your work relationship, that relationship will change. Perhaps another study and some statistics will help.

You're the average of the five people you spend the most time with. ~Jim Rohn

Rohn's quote tells us it's about the five closest people in our lives. It doesn't stop there. Nicholas Christakis and James Fowler conducted the first significant study on the breadth of social influence. According to The New England Journal of Medicine, this social network expands beyond our immediate social circle. The title abstract on their website introduces the study as follows: *The prevalence of obesity has increased substantially over the past 30 years. We performed a quantitative analysis of the nature and extent of the person-to-person spread of obesity as a possible factor contributing to the obesity epidemic.* Christakis and Fowler get the award for a study's longest and most complex abstract title.

To sum it up, your friends can make you unhealthy, but so can their friends, and so can their friends. How's that for influence? Jim Rohn addresses the first layer of relational influence. It begins with the people you associate with the most. If your friend's friends have poor eating habits that cause them to be overweight, and you also interact with them, you are twenty percent more likely to develop poor eating habits, which lead to obesity. Will your relationships change when you act in leadership regarding your eating habits? The answer is "yes." It works this way in all areas of our overall health, whether physical, intellectual, or spiritual. All three are tied together.

In my twenties, I drank like a fish on the weekends. I had several drinking buddies. We planned all our activities around being able to consume alcohol. If an event didn't allow drinking, the likelihood you'd see us there was slim and none. And slim was riding out of town on a horse. That changed when I reached my late twenties into my early thirties. Not a hard left turn, car tires screeching, and suddenly I'm on a new path, but a transition period. Someone somewhere would say it was Transitional Leadership when it was the progression of a worthy ideal.

I became involved with bodybuilding. I paired up with an old acquaintance of my brother. His name is John Allan. John practiced martial arts most of his life, ate healthier than I ever did up to that point, and he worked out consistently. But he also drank socially and had fun. My life didn't take a hard left turn. It was gradual. As my interest in a healthier lifestyle grew, the people I associated with began to change. I spent less time with my old drinking buddies. Over a few years, those friendships changed because I started working toward some worthy ideals by acting in leadership.

Whatever you believe, and how you act on those beliefs, will determine who you connect with in life, including work. Believe an authoritarian style is best for your business, then that's who ends up on top. Believe participative or transactional is the best, and those who exhibit those behaviors will hold top-level positions. Authoritarian, participative, and laissez-faire are not types of leadership. They are types of behaviors we associate with approaches to doing business in certain positions within hierarchies. You will pair up personality types most likely to exhibit those behaviors and put those people in top positions. Personality profiling has nothing to do with acting in leadership.

During my first research book, I discovered the BASIC Leadership platform. When I compared what has happened in all areas of my life, as well as in the stories written in leadership, personal development, and business books to the BASIC Leadership platform, the outcome is always the same. It defines when a person has acted in leadership and when they haven't. Getting financially healthy, physically healthy, mentally and intellectually healthy, and spiritually healthy are all worthy ideals, and your relationships will be defined and change because of your beliefs and choices.

How about Transformative Leadership? James MacGregor Burns established two well-known concepts, Transformational Leadership, and Transactional Leadership. Know what transforms? *Everything.* The entire universe and our planet constantly transform. All the separated continents we see on our global map were once a single giant land mass. That is why all the edges look like they should fit together like a puzzle. Our beliefs transform. How and why? Because we take action or do not take action, we gain insight, collaborate, and either progress toward or away from something which might or might not be a worthy ideal.

Look at the title of this chapter. If you've watched any of the Hasbro Transformer movies, you thought there might be a lesson involving the machines that can change from cars, planes, trucks, and tanks into figures who resemble people and dinosaurs, creating a better relationship between a mechanical alien species and humans. Perhaps you were expecting a lesson on Transformational Leadership under a collaborative coalition to serve others? You could be Optimus Prime. That's how easy it is to sound complex and intellectual when discussing the concept of leadership. We seem to prefer complex when simple will suffice. Simple has been around since people wrote in old Sanskrit.

CHAPTER TWENTY-TWO

Karma, Superstitions, and Schadenfreude

We continue to get things wrong, and we always will. For instance, there's no such thing as karma, at least the way it is viewed by most.

When a big game hunter gets mauled by a bear and then eaten by coyotes, it is not karma. It's...well... hilarious. "Hey Dave, watch this video. A guy is hunting a bear with his .22 pistol. What an idiot." Scream, scream, slash, slash, chomp, chomp, bear = 1, idiot = 0.

We confuse karma with superstitions and schadenfreude. I wore my pink socks every day last year and didn't get into a car accident. Therefore, wearing pink socks must prevent car accidents. I didn't wear my lucky sports jersey, and my team lost. Every time I wash my car, it rains. Those are superstitions. Washing your car doesn't make it rain, and your sports jersey has nothing to do with a team winning or losing.

When your old high school boyfriend ends up fat, bald, and divorced, you think it's because he dumped you at prom. We confuse karma with schadenfreude, a German word that means pleasure derived by someone from another person's misfortune. You got pleasure from someone else's misfortune because you feel they did you wrong. Superstitions and schadenfreude are reward and punishment mindsets based on misguided beliefs.

Karma is a Sanskrit word meaning an action, work, or deed and its effect or consequences. If a thief steals from you, and something terrible happens to them during their next theft, you say, "See, that's karma." And you would be partly correct, except we think of it in terms of "you grabbed the last waffle iron during the Black Friday buying frenzy, and God will have my revenge." Someone did you wrong, and later something bad happened to them..... *Karma*. No! Something bad is bound to happen because they are alive. Bad things happen.

Notice I didn't say, "bad things happen to us." Things happen, but not "to us." Bad things happening increase based on the true meaning of karma, which is action, effect, fate. The choices we make, and the actions we take, lead to the outcomes in our lives. Internally we know this to be true. That's why we utter phrases like, "Poop happens. Deal with it." I cleaned that up a bit, but we all know what people actually say.

People who lie a lot get caught in those lies eventually. People who steal all the time eventually get caught. The radical driver who weaves in and out of traffic going dangerously fast, and then 10 miles down the road, we see them either pulled over or in an accident is actually karma. People who constantly drive like that increase their chances of being in an accident or getting pulled over. When they cut us off in traffic, we want revenge or justice. That's schadenfreude. Even funnier is that anyone driving slower than us is an idiot, and anyone going faster than us is a maniac. The other day on the freeway, you were someone else's idiot and another person's maniac.

Have you ever noticed that anybody driving slower than you is an idiot, and anyone going faster than you is a maniac? ~George Carlin

We confuse karma with superstitions and schadenfreude, just like we confuse leadership with doing business and a position in a hierarchy. Think good thoughts, have positive beliefs, and you will act on those thoughts and beliefs. Think evil thoughts, and have negative beliefs, and you will act on those thoughts and beliefs. Action, effect, fate. Karma. Old Sanskrit contains part of the formula for defining *acting in leadership*.

Here is how life works. Humans have some unique attributes. Those attributes include the ability to reason and establish beliefs, which drive our actions and create our circumstances. However, we do not leave life up to fate when acting in leadership. Due to our unique ability to reason, to have thoughts and ideas that no other living thing on our planet possesses, we can choose to gain insight, learn from that insight, impact our beliefs, and decide to act with integrity on the positive side of the lifeline. When we do so, we are acting in leadership.

The components of the BASIC Leadership formula have been around for centuries. All someone had to do was codify them into a comprehensive platform. Karma provides us with an example of how one part of acting in leadership, in its true essence, works. Action, effect, fate. It's been around for a long time. Our beliefs drive most, if not all, of our actions. Those actions all lead to an outcome of some sort. We define those outcomes in terms of successes and non-successes. Whether positive or negative, our beliefs and actions become a habit.

CHAPTER TWENTY-THREE

Hobbits, Habits, Balance, and Change

I have made arguments for dispelling several leadership myths. A few include leadership does not require followers, leadership is not inspiration or influence, and there's no such thing as Fairness Leadership.

In chapter nineteen, I asked you to read a bit more before attempting to define leadership. Now it's time to take some action. Your objective is to define leadership and create a leadership training program. I will repeat the two options for you.

> Option 1: You get to draw from everything that exists about the concept of leadership and use it to define leadership.

> Option 2: You get to start from scratch. Under the premise that everything we know about

leadership, everything you've read, heard, or watched about leadership up to this point, does not exist.

For option one, I'll give you a few labels to get you started, and then you can choose any of the over 800 definitions of leadership and make your case for or against them as a way to define leadership. Unethical Leadership, Visionary Leadership, Servant Leadership, Decisive Leadership, Coaching Leadership, Judgmental Leadership, Bureaucratic Leadership, Commitment Leadership, Innovative Leadership, Balanced Leadership, Team-Oriented Leadership, Decision Paralysis Leadership, Collaborative Leadership, Laissez-faire Leadership, Pacesetter Leadership, Problem Solving Leadership, and of course some of the most talked about which include, Authoritative Leadership, Participative Leadership, Transactional Leadership, and Transformational Leadership.

Including followers, inspiration, and influence, that's less than 25 leadership labels or definitions. How are we doing so far? Feeling confident? Complexity already whacked you upside the head with a nerf bat? Would you rather go with option two? You can toss them all out and start from scratch. Before you make your choice, perhaps some insight into the subject of habits will help.

Bilbo, Frodo, and Samwise live in the Shire. A ring must be destroyed. Great journeys with hardships and fellowships will be required to achieve success. Collaboration with large talking trees and wizards will be necessary while battling against orcs. All made up, all mythical. Those characters and the plots mentioned refer to the *Hobbit* and *Lord of the Rings*, a series of books by J. R. R. Tolkien. It appears that we know more about a fictitious colony in middle earth than we do about why we do the same things over and over again without knowing why. We know more about Hobbits than Habits.

The Power of Habit, by Charles Duhigg, published in 2011, and *Atomic Habits*, by James Clear, published in 2018, help us to gain insight into our habits. Habits develop when we think or act consistently regarding anything. Thinking negative thoughts becomes a habit. Acting maliciously becomes a habit. Conversely, thinking positive thoughts becomes a habit, and acting with integrity becomes a habit. When we purposefully move our thoughts from negative to positive, we never reach the goal of having a positive state of mind every moment of every day. It's human nature. However, thinking positive thoughts and acting with integrity are worthy ideals. We can progress toward them, but sometimes we screw up, meaning we can also be unsuccessful at any given moment. We can begin to make doing those things a habit.

On page 148 we talked about how walking becomes a habit. We never stop progressing toward walking effectively. We do it on autopilot, subconsciously, because it has become a habit. No one ever gives up on learning to walk, yet for some reason we stop progressing toward worthy ideals in other areas. This happens because we do not do them long enough to make them a habit, and more importantly, a subconscious habit.

Most, if not all, of our actions are based on what we believe, our mindset. Our thoughts and beliefs become habits. Then we begin to act on those things subconsciously without even knowing it. They become unconscious habits.

The Biology of Belief, by Bruce Lipton, published in 2005, walks us through how this happens. The subconscious mind processes information at 40 million bits per second, and our conscious mind processes information at 40 bits per second. Therefore, our subconscious mind operates in the background, controlling 95% to 99% of our daily actions and doing this "on autopilot." Our subconscious easily overrides our conscious mind, and we are unaware that it is happening. The good news is that when we intentionally address our habits, consciously and subconsciously, we can change our path in life.

Brushing your teeth and praying every day are habits that must be developed. Complaining and being negative are habits a person forms. Getting up late, rushing around, and then dangerously weaving in and out of traffic becomes a habit. There is nothing complicated about habits. We must be aware of how we act out of habit, and then put in time and effort to direct to make a change. Developing good habits is a worthy ideal. Remember what karma truly means? Action, effect, fate.

Until you make the unconscious conscious, it will direct your life, and you will call it fate. ~Carl Jung

We discussed personality profiles in chapter twenty-one, mentioning Carl Jung. Jung was a Swiss psychiatrist and psychoanalyst who founded analytical psychology. Jung was telling us about subconscious habits back in the early 1900s. This is not new folks. Jung's quote combines Karma and habits. Why don't more people know about how habits and our subconscious mind work?

Because we have made incredible advancements in our information technologies, two things have occurred. First, our access to information is the easiest it's ever been in any society. Second, so much information exists that one has difficulty sorting through it all. The second part dramatically outweighs the first part.

One subject, habits, has hundreds of books to choose from. Where would you have started if I did not provide those three resources? One of them didn't even have "habits" in the title. How do you know they are resources with reliable information? How many other resources would you want to look at to help you define leadership? Are these three resources about personal development or leadership? Would Decisive Leadership be the answer? Perhaps the book *The Paradox of Choice* by Barry Schwartz, published in 2004, will help you with your Decision Paralysis Leadership. There's no such thing as Decision Paralysis Leadership.

How about Balance Leadership? During my twelve-plus years of bodybuilding, I lost count of the number of times people would ask me how much I could bench press. I would always respond with, "I have no idea." Because I had the physique of a well-developed bodybuilder, they would look at me like, "How could you not know how much you can bench press?"

What I did was body shaping for symmetry, for balance. Frank Zane, a three-time Mr. Olympia in the 1970s, was also known as "The Chemist" due to his bachelor's degree in science. Zane's approach to bodybuilding was the catalyst that created a shift from simply getting massive to creating symmetry. Take a gander at photos of some of the bodybuilders in that era. Frank Zane, Lee Haney, Arnold Schwarzenegger, and Shawn Ray dominated through symmetry. Judges looked for balance as well as mass. My worthy ideal wasn't seeing how much I could bench press. It was achieving symmetry. Acting in leadership regarding finances, health, and relationships is the beginning of progressing toward symmetry in life.

Look up the label Balance Leadership and tell us what you find. Are the articles primarily about business? How many different descriptions and approaches did you see? Which one would you choose to define when a person is acting in leadership? I have a better question. Have you, or anyone you know, ever achieved balance?

That question is hard to answer because we cannot agree on what a balanced life means, nor can a person measure it. In 2011 Matthew Kelly published his book *Off Balance: Getting Beyond the Work-Life Balance Myth.* Work-life balance is a myth. No one I know has ever achieved this mythical balance, yet executive coaches talk about how it is a goal for their organizational clients.

If you haven't noticed, balance and symmetry are synonyms. We can find the two words as labels attached to leadership. That's how easy it is to raise the level of complexity. We might be able to create balance using a scale. We can come close to creating symmetry when shaping our bodies. However, in life or business, not so much. What are you trying to balance? There is no such thing as Balance Leadership.

What about Change Leadership? In July of 2000, Malcolm Higgs and Deborah Rowland released an analysis paper defining change leadership. "Change leadership is the ability to influence and enthuse others through personal advocacy, vision, and drive, and to access resources to build a solid platform for change." There's a mouthful. Are they right? Wouldn't a solid platform for change be something constant, a process one could follow, and it doesn't change? Is their description a long-winded version of an oxymoron such as civil war, jumbo shrimp, or virtual reality? There's nothing civil about any war, and anything virtual, by definition, isn't real. Can there be a solid platform for change? Interestingly, this article, and many others that address Change Leadership, are published in a journal aptly named the *Journal of Change Management*. Why not the Journal of Change Leadership?

Do you know why I hit myself in the head with a hammer? Because it feels so good when I stop.

Do you know what changes? Everything. The weather changes. Our planet has gone from ice ages to warmer climates and back into ice ages repeatedly over the millennia. Every day you and I change in some way. One quick google search gives us the four steps of Change Leadership, the 3 Cs of Change Leadership, and a long laundry list of other attributes for being a change leader. The BASIC Leadership platform addresses constant change, moving from one component to the next because life consists of continuous change. What is the one thing that we can prove is constant? Change is the only constant. There is no such thing as Change Leadership.

Why did that last paragraph seem so familiar? Because in chapter twenty, we talked about Transformational Leadership. Look up the synonyms for change, and you will find transform. Look up the synonyms for transform, and you will find change. Yet we have two different leadership labels as if somehow they are not one and the same. Perhaps we should try to balance the two labels in an attempt to create symmetry. I could easily write a small book about how Change Leadership is different than Transformative Leadership and sound very convincing.

Perhaps we should all operate under Autonomous Leadership. Autonomy is the right or condition of self-government. It's about freedom and self-rule. Look up Autonomous Leadership and see what people are discussing. The most common argument about what constitutes autonomy? An employee's ability to set their schedule. It's not autonomy if a person has to be given permission to make that choice. That's not autonomy;

it's flexibility in a work schedule and only done with permission from someone up the hierarchy. That's just business. Walk into work tomorrow and tell them you want to operate under Autonomous Leadership, and you'll be setting your work schedule. Tell them you are self-governing through freedom and see how that conversation goes.

When writing about leadership myths, coming up with ideas for coaching platforms becomes incredibly easy. The fun part is that I have the autonomy to be transformative, creating a balance between serious and silly things that organizations would pay me to present to their executives under a collaborative effort (see what I did there?). And I'd be getting paid for being innovative while influencing educated people in high-level positions to do embarrassing things.

I call the one about balance, "The Flamingo." During a leadership training session, I let everyone know we're going to talk about Balance Leadership, then get all the executives standing on one leg to see if they have balance. I would get them to put out their arms to see if that helps (it won't, but that's how you get people to look more like giant birds).

Most, if not all, would struggle and even have the appearance of flapping their wings. Then I would have them stand close and hold onto one another, lift one leg, and show how supporting each other creates balance. I would then tie it into teamwork or some random concept by uttering phrases like "Teamwork Makes the Dreamwork."

I can take a group of highly educated executives and get them to hop on one leg attempting to imitate flamingos, and they would pay me for it. Now if I can only come up with a way to get them all dressed in pink. The flamingo exercise is not much different than teams of executives putting marshmallows on the tops of long toothpick-shaped sticks or tying their wrists together and challenging them to perform a Houdini separation trick in the name of leadership.

How is your project of defining leadership progressing? I was going to write something about Procrastination Leadership to help you, but I never got around to doing the research.

CHAPTER TWENTY-FOUR

Leadership:
A Broken System

In 2008, over two million homeowners, 2,330,483 to be exact, filed for foreclosure. That number continued to increase for the next two years before it began to taper off. The headlines splashed all over news outlets, written in articles, and still misrepresented today across the world wide web is that a band of rebel loan officers were at fault. Greedy, immoral, and untrained, they created this mess. That narrative will continue until we learn the real story, just like the story of David and Goliath. The real story, in this case, is that systems drive behaviors.

When the system is broken, we get undesirable behaviors. The mortgage meltdown resulted from a system that drove behaviors that damaged an entire economy, which impacted us globally. Those at the top of hierarchies create broken systems and then blame everyone but those who made the system. Humans get an A for proficiency in this arena.

How does a financial meltdown in the housing market occur? By creating a broken system. Banks may initially lend their own money to a person who buys a home, but they then transfer those loans to other entities. Banks take a group of mortgages, bundle them together as an asset, and transition them from being owned by the bank to owned by investors. Those investors then carry the risk if people default on those loans; at least, that's what one might assume. After all, someone has to carry the burden under Risk Leadership. That's what those who talk about Risk Leadership tell others.

Starting in the 1970s, national mortgage agencies began their rise. The terms Ginnie Mae, Fannie Mae, and Freddie Mac sound like your cute little grandma or your kookie uncle helping you get a home loan. Those clever-sounding names refer to the Government National Mortgage Association (GNMA, aka Ginnie Mae), Federal National Mortgage Association (FNMA, aka Fannie Mae), and Federal Home Loan Mortgage Association (FHLMC, aka Freddie Mac).

Congress chartered Fannie and Freddie to support the U.S. home finance system. Fannie Mae and Freddie Mac do this by purchasing mortgages from lenders, packaging them into securities, and selling the securities to investors. GNMA's original mission? Expand funding for mortgages insured or guaranteed by other federal agencies. Protecting investors from loss is one of the attributes of these programs.

Investors invest to make money. And investors at this level, hundreds of millions or even billions of dollars, expect significant returns, not little ones. Big returns diminish quickly if the risk is high and can rapidly result in losses. In this case, the risk is homeowners who default on their loans.

When a person goes back and looks at banking and homeownership from the 1700s through the 1940s, it is easy to see why banks and investors hesitate to play in this arena without some protection. There are only two options for banks to address home loan risk.

One: Set conditions where the borrower has to put some of their own money toward the purchase so they have some skin in the game, meaning they have something substantial to lose. Putting 20% down was the norm, and it had to be from your own money. Combine the 20% down with a borrower's ability to show stability in generating an income that can *easily* support making the payment, then the risk is at an acceptable level.

Two: Shift the risk out of the banks hands and into someone else's hands. If you're a bank that lends money, this one looks pretty darn good.

Under option one, the risk can be high even with the money down and stability factors. I will spare you a long history lesson but go back and look at what happened to farm loans during the dust bowl era. Banks lost their butts.

Securitization is a shift of the risk from one entity to another under the Fannie Mae and Freddie Mac programs. They are taking a group of mortgages and transferring them from being owned by the bank to be owned by investors. The government-backed organizations protect against losses. What would those involved in mortgage-backed securities do if the banks and the investors were now protected against losses? Well, we watch what the government, banks, and investors team up to do next. They create risky mortgage programs. If things go wrong, everyone gets to walk away. And they did, leaving society holding the bag. They created a broken system, which then lead to the big "Bail Out."

Have you ever heard of "sub-prime" loans? How about a "no-doc" loan? A prime mortgage is a loan available to a borrower with high credit scores and assets such as savings or other investments well above the average person. That borrower can put money down and prove they have enough income to make home loan payments consistently and on time (20% down and stability in income). The risk is minimized for banks or other lenders. These loans are referred to as "A-paper" or "prime." They are prime, like an excellent cut of steak; they are the good stuff lenders prefer. A-paper borrowers get the best interest rates. Based on this description, you can quickly guess what "subprime" implies.

Sub-prime refers to loan programs that allow borrowers with very sketchy credit and little or no assets to get a home loan. Credit scores for A-paper loans are generally 720 and above. Sub-prime programs allowed people with as low as 540 credit scores to get a loan. No more 20% down either. A borrower could get a sub-prime loan with only a few thousand dollars out of their own pocket, and even that money could come from a family member. Take a few minutes to research what behaviors a person has to exhibit financially to get a 540 credit score and, as an investor or bank, you'd run from that situation. That is unless you were protected.

Loans used to require a person to show how much money they made and proof that they had assets. These subprime and specialty programs reached the point where a person could show up without providing any documentation, and they could get a loan for one or two hundred thousand dollars more than they could truly afford. They called these "no-doc loans."

These specialty programs created a home buying frenzy. Anyone wanting, needing, or willing to sell their home would get multiple offers. In many cases, the offers would exceed the listing price for the home, which then drove home values upward. From 2000 to 2007, home prices increased an average of 100%, and in some areas, as much as 200%. And that happened with interest rates beginning at over 8% in 2000, and only going down to around 6% for most of the decade. Think about that for a minute. Interest rates at 6 to 8% and people were in a buying frenzy.

Folks, this overall approach to homeownership is the epitome of a broken system just waiting to come crashing down, and it did. Home loan defaults began to rise, investors panicked, home loan finance organizations locked their doors and ran for the hills, home values plummeted, and it all crashed.

The system drove the behaviors from top to bottom. Those at the top created the system, then, as history always shows us, they tried to blame everyone else, most specifically those on the front lines.

We've done the same thing with the concept of leadership. We've created a broken system. A system that drives behaviors unbecoming of leadership in its true essence. It hasn't crashed, but it's doing damage.

Leadership: A Broken System

What people will try to tell you is that the mortgage meltdown is much too complex for the average person to understand. Some will take you down a rabbit hole into Alice's wonderland, introducing you to magical characters who played a part. We use complexity to scare people away from simple truths. What is happening with leadership is as easy to explain as the mortgage meltdown, and the broken system of how we refer to leadership is driving the wrong behaviors.

As the industrialization of the United States began its rapid climb, leadership became associated with doing business and attached to positions in hierarchies. Because we identified it as a position rather than what it is in its true essence, its basic form, we attached hundreds and hundreds of labels to the concept attempting to figure it out. These labels included negatively based behaviors such as the unethical actions of those at the top levels of hierarchies. The level of complexity rose at a staggering rate, leading to confusion and uncertainty. That complexity has caused more problems than solutions, including conflicting messages about what constitutes leadership and the appearance of a lack of leaders.

The concept of leadership is an invention, just as business management is an invention. We invented business management during the industrialization of the United States. We took farmers and other craftsmen and craftswomen from many different trades. We brought them into factories where they now had to work in large groups of people under the watchful eye of a supervisor who would hold them accountable for mass-producing consumer goods. Work conditions mixed dangerous machinery and a fast-paced environment with complex bureaucratic systems.

Leadership entered the picture after the behaviors associated with management set in. We already had a system under which companies and organizations operated. That system was, and still is, "business management." Then came leadership, another invention. We began to call those at the top of hierarchies leaders rather than use their actual titles, such as CEO, and then assumed that this is also where leadership exists.

When someone at the top acted in a manner inconsistent with leadership in its true essence, we created labels such as unethical leadership, which should never have existed in the first place, just like subprime mortgages should never have existed. It's as if Leadership and Home Financing were standing face to face, a mirror image of one another.

We drove complexity to levels beyond comprehension, then told people they were incapable of understanding any of it, leading to a multi-billion dollar industry of fads. All this time, its simplicity is lying on the floor right in front of us, waiting for us to look down and see it. Perhaps if we had not learned to walk, we would have noticed it when we had to crawl over it.

Those who created the mortgage debacle operated under the misguided premise that homeownership is a right. That's not true. A person has to earn it. Owning a home is different than having a place to live. Those who created these "lacking common sense" programs told people that this would increase the number of people who would own a home, especially those labeled as "disenfranchised." They stood behind a false protective wall of empathy under the premise of "we're doing it to help others. We're the good guys looking out for those in need."

In 1983 homeowner participation was at 65.6%. As of 2016, homeowner participation was still just over 65%. Any new innovation or new efforts to create financing options for home purchasers since 1983 have had a total impact of zip, zilch, and nada, except for creating a financial meltdown on a global scale.

Unlike the mortgage meltdown, the leadership debacle happened slowly and has not caused a sudden societal crash. However, the current broken system of defining leadership has damaged society. We've been told that leadership is a position in a hierarchy, when in fact, it is right there for the taking by anyone and has nothing to do with any hierarchy.

Tell people that when they get followers, they will be a leader; then, by default, we will have more leaders. But no one admits to or wants to be a follower. Tell people that when they can influence people, they will become a leader, then by default, we will have more leaders acting in leadership. Instead, we have so-called leaders influencing people to do things unbecoming of leadership. If the current system has merit, why do we not have more leaders acting in leadership? If you think we have more leaders under these false premises, can you prove it? We have people running around trying to influence people, just like we had people originating no-doc loans. Then when they do either, and the system fails, we blame them, then create more fads.

Please present your case for not having enough leaders of a specific ethnicity or gender. Be careful when you begin to talk in terms of hierarchies. If you do, you're arguing that there are not enough, or a disproportionate number of, CEOs, Generals, Senators, Head Coaches, News Anchors, or any other title held by a specific ethnicity or gender. That has nothing to do with acting in leadership and being a leader. Ok, go!

Start a company, build an organization, and hold a position at the top of that hierarchy, and you can now be part of the leadership team, yet you can't leadership anything. Saying that to be a leader, one must have followers, that leadership is influence, that leadership is inspiration, and the abundance of other attempts to define leadership have had the same impact on creating leaders as the steps taken to increase homeownership over the last forty plus years, nada, zilch, zip. We've been rearranging the chairs on the deck of the Titanic while the ship continues to take on water.

We wanted to know why so many people defaulted on their home loans, and now we want to understand why more people aren't leaders acting in leadership. It's ok if you're grinning and even chuckling right now. It is humorous how we create systems that drive odd behaviors, then scratch our heads wondering why people behave the way they do. We have done the same thing with our tax system. Complexity beyond belief, and most, if not all of it, is designed to drive specific behaviors. We create complex broken systems that drive the wrong behaviors, usually under the misguided belief that we are helping others.

Instead of showing people how to be financially responsible, we said, "don't worry about that, we'll manipulate the system, so you don't have to act in leadership. Here's some money for a home you cannot afford." Likewise, we give leadership negative labels such as unethical leadership, then refer to corrupt and dishonest CEOs, senators, and coaches as leaders.

Neither has turned out well. Homeownership hasn't gone up, and we constantly hear that we lack leaders. Leadership and the number of leaders have not increased under the current system. There are no stats to back up that statement. Instead, look around and determine if what you see in the behaviors at work, in government, or your local community would be labeled as *acting in leadership*.

What's sad is that while subprime loans went away, the banking industry and investors continue to try to devise ways to make getting home loans easier, twisting and manipulating an already broken system. With well over 800 definitions, I wonder how long we'll continue to operate under the current broken and misguided systems of defining leadership and, of course, continue to manipulate it under the false premise that leadership is a position in a hierarchy.

The obscure we see eventually. The completely apparent takes longer. ~Edward Murrow

I have defined when a person is acting in leadership, which makes you a leader only while doing so, but we will never be able to come up with one all-encompassing definition for leadership. Leadership isn't influence or inspiration, does not require a person to have followers, and leadership isn't a position in any hierarchy. There is no such thing as white leadership, black leadership, Hispanic leadership, Asian leadership, or any other gender or ethnicity-based leadership. There is certainly no such thing as political leadership, and there is absolutely no such thing as business leadership. There is only leadership in its true essence, a state which a person can only achieve by acting in leadership.

Take The Challenge

What I present in this book is my opinion based on my research. I do not proclaim to be correct. I claim to have decoded a formula for when a person is acting in leadership. True wisdom is knowing that you know nothing or very little in relation to the vast amount on information that exists.

The only true wisdom is in knowing you know nothing.
~Socrates

Based on this newly uncovered formula, I am heading up a movement to pushback on most of the current definitions of leadership. My objective is to address the root causes associated with the concept of leadership, not treat the symptoms. You, the reader, have the ability to participate. I challenge you to define leadership. I created an interactive platform where you can share your definition with other readers.

Go to <u>www.scottmcarter.com/challenge</u>